SAY ANYTHING

> Good, kind and non-bullshit things to say when you don't know what to say.

FIONA JEFFERIES

Copyright © 2022 by Fiona Jefferies

All rights reserved. No part of this publication may be reproduced, distributed, or transmitted in any form or by any means, including photocopying, recording, or other electronic or mechanical methods, without the prior written permission of the author/publisher, except in the case of brief quotations embodied in critical reviews and certain other noncommercial uses permitted by copyright law.

For permission requests, write to the author at: fionajefferies.com.au

Say Anything /Fiona Jefferies—1st ed.

ISBN Paperback: 978-0-6456284-0-1
ISBN Hardcover: 978-0-6456284-1-8

DEDICATION

This book is dedicated to G, my sister Emma, and all the fine[1] people in my life who taught me to have better conversations, say words that matter, and level the fuck up.

INTRODUCTION

"STOP hurting her. Your behaviour is NOT acceptable," I spat the words at the man-mountain. I'd inserted myself and the shittiest broom in all of creation between this hulking brute and the woman's forearm on which he had a vice-like grip. I was on the Upper West Side in New York, helping clean up in the aftermath of Hurricane Sandy. I had the crucial task of cleaning up the detritus and bloated rat bodies that had bubbled up from the storm surge. The broom issued to me was an actual caricature of a witch's broom used at Halloween dress-ups to clean the area's streets and parks. As a cleaning device, it was laughable. As a weapon of choice, it was only slightly more effective.

This rattiest broom in all of creation, my bravura and strident words had no bargaining power. People brushed by us, and a fight between a couple intercepted by a woman and her witches broom draws zero attention in the post-Sandy come down.

Time for shit to get real. "I'm an AUSTRALIAN!" This caused the brute some pause.

"THIS WILL NOT STAND". His fury subsided, replaced by a look of bewilderment.

"IT'S AGAINST THE ANZUS TREATY[2]!" Got him! If faced with a powerful enemy, confuse the shit out of them.

I see my chance. "YOU THERE!" I thrust my spindly broom of sticks lashed to an undersized length of dowel at a stranger with a phone at his ear, "CALL THE POLICE".

The bully let go of the woman's arm. The woman tearfully pulls away, calling him names under her breath. Someone called the police. And I'm standing on a corner of the Upper West Side with a rubbish bag stuffed full of plastic bottles, takeaway containers and dead rats at my feet with my ineffectual broom still shielding the woman.

Not for the first time, I realised that sometimes you just need to say anything. The words don't have to be quote-worthy or memorable; you just need to say something. The comic broom and I were no match for this furious fella who was physically hurting another, but with words, I stood a better chance. Sure, I've thought of SO MANY wittier or sicker burns I could have said. But at the time, the combination of tapping into the universal love/curiosity of Australians topped with the casual mention of the ANZUS treaty (WTF is that?!?) was enough to break the moment and short circuit his anger.

This example shows that those words don't need to be perfect. They need only to be from the heart, unique in the moment and delivered with intention. Of course, if you find yourself clutching a broom, so much the better.

In the following pages, I want to give you some good words to say in all situations, not just ones with dead rats stacked up at your feet. These are not examples you need to learn by heart but ones that will inspire you to think more intentionally about the words you say. Words are so powerful—they can comfort, destroy, lift, invoke joy and start wars. Be that person that is thoughtful with their words. Use them for good and not spark international dust-ups that see missiles launched and refugees on the march to somewhere that offers peace.

I'd like to think I've said smart and helpful words to people over the years, but I know I could and can do better. This book is for all of us to recognise the true power of our words and be confident communicators and all-around good humans.

CONTENTS

Introduction 5
A Is For Arseholes 11
A Is Also For Ageing 14
A Is Also For Ageing Parents 17
A Is Also For Appearance 21
B Is For Body 24
B Is Also For "The Business" 29
C Is For Commitments 33
D Is For Disasters, Natural Style! 37
D Is Also For Divorce and Breakups 46
E Is For "Eh...Wait...What?!?! 50
F Is For Friends 58
F Is Also For Freakouts 63
G Is For Giving 67
H Is For Hairy Situations 72
I Is For Illness 77
J Is For Jealousy 85
J Is For Jobs 89
K Is For Kindness 92
L Is For The Loss Of A Loved One 96
M Is For Medical Stuff 101
M Is Also For Miscellaneous 106
N Is For No Words 110
O Is For Ownership Or Owner-Shit
(Own Your Own Shit And Leave Others To Do Similarly) . . 113
P Is For Pregnant Pauses 119
Q Is For Quitting 123
R Is For Raging 127
S Is For Singled Out 132
T Is For "The Crib" 138
U Is For "You Got Me Matey?" Is For 152
V Is For Victories...And The Humblebrag . . 157
W Is For Workplace 163

X Is For X Rated	175
Y Is For Young Folk	180
Z Is For Zealots	185
TL:DR	189
Final Words	193
Additional Resources	195
Acknowledgements	201
Endnotes	203

A IS FOR ARSEHOLES

"GO FUCK A PIG!"

It's a truth universally acknowledged that you'll encounter arseholes as you move about the world. Sometimes they're elusive, and cream cakes and fluffy bunnies will colour your view of the world. Other times, they are packed six deep on an airless train carriage, and there's no escaping from their wretchedness.

Recently in another stretch of Livin' La Vida Covid Lockdown, I was striding about the neighbourhood having a stupid little walk for my stupid little mental health and lo, an Arsehole sideswiped me. I'd been breathing the fresh air of the free when I spotted another human hurtling toward me, and I secured my mask over my face.

As we passed one another, he spat, "Really, REALLY?!? DO YOU THINK I HAVE COVID?!? IT'S ALL A GOVERNMENT CONSPIRACY, AND SMALL BUSINESSES ARE BEING RUINED, AND IT'S BILL GATES FAULT!"

Look, I'm not denying that Bill Gates has to atone for all the Microsoft Word updates that always seem to occur when you're balls deep in a bang-it-out-session with only minutes to spare before a critical presentation, but it's a stretch to parlay shitty software to a nefarious global mind-control plan.

And I told him so.

'GO FUCK A PIG".

Upon reflection, while I admired the succinctness of my comeback, it was unbefitting my usually sunny disposition.

* * *

Sometimes low-brow is what's required. I've nothing against the juvenile, expletive-laden response, but there are other ways to verbally administer the equivalent of the thwat of a tea towel across the back of the shins.

Such as:

"Don't get me started on the national rugby teammate; they're not human!"[3] This non-sensical approach sees the outrageous statement issued and then rides out to meet it with the absurd to disarm the opponent.

"Bill Gates is my cousin, dude—step off!" Just as people feel emboldened on the socials to talk smack about people they don't know and have zero risk of encountering in real life, if you name-check the vilified person and provide a personal association, sometimes it's enough to make the offender know they are dehumanising a real live person and it can give them pause for thought.

"Nope, not true, but you have a good day nonetheless". This calls out the misinformation and lies but also sees the person behind the statement—and wishes them well all the same.

Say Nothing. Literally do not make eye contact, do not engage, do not dignify their arsehole-ery with a response. Silence can also be a response.

A IS ALSO FOR AGEING

I recently celebrated my 50th birthday.

And I hated it.

Oh, sure, the day will be filled with love, heartfelt wishes and celebrations, but it was totally ruined by a number of birthday cards having a message that went something like:

Roses are red
Mucus is green
How about you hide yourself away,
Because being 50 really is obscene

The fucking nerve of these cards makes ageing into something to be ashamed of. I'm still kicking while so many others have never had the chance to reach 50 years of strolling the earth because of war, disease, poverty and parts of space junk crushing you to death while you sleep.

I'm fifty, but I'm also a little bit older and a little bit bolder.

I ask for what I want.

I advocate for the rights of others.

I'm in very rude health.

I now wear crop tops for the first time in my life because I'm all out of fuck's-to-give[4].

And at 50, I'm also interested and interesting, and I have a deep abiding hatred for birthday cards with cuddly teddy bears on the cover holding a sign that says, "Awwww, I can't bear that you're fifty".

GET BENT.

※ ※ ※

Here are some go-to's you might want to use as your loved one's age:

"Hey, happy birthday! What are you looking forward to in the next birthday year ahead?" I love open-ended questions, partly because I'm nosy but also because people love to talk about themselves. These open-ended questions allow you to kick back and let someone else do the heavy lifting conversation-wise while you get to learn more about your person... winning!

"I know this is a milestone birthday for you. So how's it landing for you?" This is helpful if you're not sure how the person views this milestone, and you're giving them the floor to speak honestly about their feelings.

"Is there a way we can mark your special day?" My fabulous Aunty Christine decided that she no longer wanted to mark

birthdays with a lot of fuss a few years ago. She'd prefer the day to pass peacefully, with a phone call or a card, but please spare her from another present she does not need or some off-key singing. It starts up a chorus from the local dogs, doncha' know?

For some feel-good vibes no matter what age you are, I'd suggest following the divine Susan Hyatt, epic coach and author of "Bare". The book is a "fuck you" to diet culture and celebrating yourself. Susan is approaching her fifties with a joyous heart and fearless spirit that is inspirational.

A IS ALSO FOR AGEING PARENTS

As I've reached the 50-year milestone, my parents are also ageing. While the most I'm grappling with is sickeningly juvenile teddy bear cards, their challenges are so much more diverse and complex.

Many adult kids are having conversations with their parents, grandparents and loved ones about ageing in place, end-of-life care plans and what quality of life looks like for them.

For my mum, the Covid lockdowns curtailed her regular outings for lunch with friends and shopping for handicraft supplies (honestly, the woman is jonesing for cross-stitch Aida)—and the opportunity for passive exercise and daily movement evaporated. She now has a lesser range of mobility than BC (Before Covid), and she'd raised the issue of not being able to lift her feet even to step up from a single step into her home.

Before I rushed in with the solutions to the issues and being a good and caring child, I had the good sense to check myself and ask her first what her plans were. I've heard my mum talk many times about wanting determination over her life for as long as possible. So I decided to ask her about what she'd noticed with her reduction in mobility and if she'd considered any solutions.

Turns out she had some ideas like seeking in-home support and continuing her twice-weekly Physiotherapy sessions. We also discussed it with my sister and came up with the idea of custom-made ramps for the home so she could use her walker for greater stability when getting up steps, no matter how minor they might seem. Without having a discussion with mum about her needs and ideas, I would've rushed in to be the saviour that mum didn't ask for and being a tedious know-it-all. And that would have pissed my mum off. She might be old, but she still knows what's best for her and can advocate for her needs and wishes.

I'd advise doing a two-step plan to have sensitive conversations around death and end-of-life plans. You don't want to drop the "So, what're your thoughts on assisted dying?" As you stand in front of the dairy cabinet during your weekly shop. Everyone needs some time to warm up to the conversation, so find a quiet moment to raise the topic of the conversation and ask when would be a good time to talk about it. They might be keen to kick on right then and there, or they might be a more appropriate time for them. Such as on the back verandah eating delicious chocolate mousse from that dairy cabinet.

Here are some conversations that were helpful when talking to my parents about ageing:

"I know this can be a sensitive topic, but I was wondering if you'd like to talk about your end-of-life care plan, so we know what your wishes are when the time comes." As we're all

getting older and in many countries and jurisdictions, there are debates around assisted dying being held; it's a great move to schedule some time with your loved ones to discuss end-of-life plans, power of attorney and details of the will. It's not a topic we're gagging to have, but it's worth broaching so there's clarity around your loved one's wishes, and it will help when the day does come, and you can focus and the care of your person and not trying to ferret around the house looking for their will or agonising over if they wanted to be revived.

"I hope this day is in the distant future, but I'd like to raise the topic of your funeral. I'd like to talk about this even though it's a very sad topic. I want to be sure that I honour you in a way that is in line with your wishes. Have you thought about how you'd like you'd like to be remembered at your funeral?" The death of our loved ones is an emotional time, but you don't need to overlay that with added stress trying to decide if they want to be revived, have their organs donated or want all Cat Stevens songs banned at their funeral. (Readers, this is 100% me. I hate all Cat Steven's music with a passion bordering on the unhinged. Do not "Peace Train" anywhere near me, even in death. I mean, the whole concept of a Peace Train is deeply flawed. ANYONE who has ever been on a train knows that's PEACE in absentia. There are substances of unknown origin on most of the seats, and windows have been scratched so deeply with keys that the only thing you can see out of them is some etching of "Jerry waz' ere" with a crude sketch version of his dick and balls. There's a stench that came from the bowels of Satan himself. Some jackass is listening to a Joe Rogan podcast SANS earbuds, and now the entire carriage gets to listen to that ding-a-long sprout rubbish that's offensive to 100% of the carriage inhabitants. Peace Train, my arse).

"Have you considered any in-home care support to assist you in living more comfortably?" If they say yes, please, for

the love of small furry animals, don't leave the conversation there. Offer to do some research with them to see what's available, as the mountain of help and information out there can be overwhelming to navigate. If they decline, acknowledge this and let them know you're available to chat if they change their mind. Just because it's a no, for now doesn't mean it's a no forever.

If they say "no, not really", you could offer a few suggestions. For instance, you could say, *"My friend Rosie recently hired someone to come by the house and help out with cleaning, cooking, and yard work for just a couple of hours each week. Is that something we could look into?"* Propose ideas—help with cleaning, errands, decluttering, and organising. See if any of your suggestions are attractive to them or spark ideas of their own.

"Are you concerned about any aspect of your care, well-being or health?" This open-ended question is gold. You might think that you have a firm handle on how your loved one is faring, but with a question like this, you could uncover something that has been troubling them or they have been looking for an opportunity to raise. Have your poker face at the ready if they come back with, "Yes, I want to talk about my Bitcoin account". And tell them, "Bitcoin is so over, and it's all about Ethereum and NFTs these days. Jeez, everyone knows that!" LOL.

A IS ALSO FOR APPEARANCE

Carly Findlay (recipient of the prestigious Order of Australia Medal, don't cha know) is an educator, writer, activist and speaker. She has the best and most wondrous rainbow-hued collection of wearable art (such glorious creations can't be categorised as jewellery) and fashion. And she has Ichthyosis, a rare skin and hair disorder. This is the least bit interesting part of Carly's story. Still, one she's forced on a daily basis to address and provide insights on what she and so many others encounter living with facial and appearance differences.

A recent example Carly shared on her social media was spotting two young kids at a fuel stop staring at her. Carly smiled at them and carried on with refuelling her car. One of the children told her, "she scared of you, she's scared of you!" While pointing at the other child. Carly responded that she found that troubling and did not want to scare people. She made the point to the mother of the kids that you have to teach kids not to be scared. Not unsurprisingly, this whole encounter was very upsetting for Carly, as it would be for anyone that was openly told, even by a child, that their appearance was causing fear.

Carly has often stated in books, social media posts, and activism that the work to provide a safe and inclusive community is not the burden of the disabled or the appearance / facially diverse folk. The work is to be done by the rest of the community by talking with kids and each other, countering harmful or misplaced views on what people "should" look like in the very narrow definition that society holds.

Many of us now watch our language around how we comment—or don't comment—on another's body. "You're so pretty!" As a complement to my nieces has been swapped out for "I love that skirt—I bet you can twirl like a fairy in it". Changes in the body shape of a friend I have not seen in a while are met with "Hey, it's been too long since I saw you catch me up. What's new with you?" A good opener like this will set the tone for someone to share any significant news relating to weight if they feel comfortable to do so. It's much preferable to "You've lost a tonne of weight—are you battling an illness or on a special diet?!?" Honey, no, comments on appearance are fraught so steer clear and only comment with care if the other party raises it first.

I've also learned that trying to be overly concerned and mindful can also lead to needle-drag moments. One of my nieces, when shopping with me, commented on a man nearby with a walking stick and a half-leg prosthesis. She exclaimed, "What's going on with him, Aunty Noni?" I then launched into 127 ways that a man might lose part of his leg and how we needed to be mindful that we're all unique and isn't great to see so many different types of people out on a beautiful spring morning. "It's not that, Aunty Noni. It's his cap," my niece interrupted my TED X Talk. In my rush to deliver a sermon, I totally missed the cap that the gentleman was wearing that had "I'm a horny little Devil" emblazoned on it. "Oh... well. Um." I searched for something to salvage this conversation "I think he's into roses. Or alternate religions". She was not convinced, and I was left with a good lesson to dig deeper on an initial query rather than relying on my assumptions.

A dear friend gave me this piece of gold when hanging with the kids: "What do *you* think that means?" Her mum used to use this one with her when she was very little and helped her mum steer the conversation accordingly. If I'd used this tip, I would have learned that we needed to talk about men and their social-sexual solicitations and less about differences in appearance.

I want to take up Carly's challenge for us to have better conversations with kids and each other about how not to be shocked, scared or hurtful when we meet someone with differences in appearances and here's my crack at it:

If someone mentions the appearance of another and is curious, you could say, *"Yes, but what else do you notice about them?"* For example, you might refer to their happy smile, a pair of killer heels they are wearing, a decorated walking aid or the shiny coat of the assistance animal they are with.

If someone mentions they are fearful or disgusted by the appearance of another, you can counter this with, *"There's nothing to be scared or disgusted by. They are a human being like you and me. If we were them, we'd be heartbroken to hear that people felt this way about us."*

If someone is openly staring, laughing or talking smack about another's appearance, this can be stopped dead with *"We don't do that {name the behaviour}. This is not kind or caring. That behaviour {name it again so they are clear what's being called out} is just not on."* We can't let hurtful and demeaning comments

B IS FOR BODY

I had a fuck of a time writing this entry.

Every time I decided to write, I was nervy and easily distracted. I wrote a line and then deleted it. This is a highly charged topic for me. Every day since my first day in kindergarten, when I was called fat by a 5-year-old girl with better pigtails than me and a body so much smaller than my own, I had judged my body and deemed it ugly and un-conforming.

My thighs were too big and they rubbed against each other

My stretch marks were visible beneath my bikini line and were so gross.

My breast was too small to suit my frame.

My upper arms were toneless as a windsock

My lower belly was bulging over my jeans belt.

And these were the better comments I made about my body.

There's a lot of truth in the saying: "don't worry about what others think of your body. Everyone is too busy obsessing over their own". I know from my own experience that since that bruising first day in kindergarten and having been labelled as the fat kid, I want to make damn sure that I have said the most hateful things about my body, so I'm no longer surprised or alarmed by their words because I've said the vilest things to myself already.

With such a personal and fraught topic that is bodies, what could I possibly offer as advice on saying something helpful and kind?

Here's the top-line advice from someone who's been on the other end of so many others' comments about my body: *please don't say anything.*

Think someone is pregnant? Shut that pie hole until they announce the news themselves. Then feel free to release the confetti bomb, buy up cute onesies and up your lego building skills.

Notice that a mate has either put on weight or suddenly lost it? Keep it to yourself until they mention it. I guarantee the person sporting the weight loss/gain is acutely aware of it and does not need you to bring it to their attention, no matter how much you think it might be of interest to them.

Haven't seen a friend for a while, and you notice that their previous normal-looking body has been replaced with bulging muscles and abs you can grate cheese on? Zip it. Zip it good. If they raise the topic of their body transformation, then by all means ask about their reps, training schedule and could salted caramel cheesecake be considered a protein-dense meal? (Reader, it can)

✶ ✶ ✶

Not commenting on someone's body before being invited to is the gold standard. But if you're invited by someone to offer your opinion, make like the crew from Queer Eye and be kind and positive.

For example:

If a family member asks if you think they've put on weight recently while tugging on their waistband, you can say, *"Hmmm, well, I've been pretty involved inventing a new cheese / playing with Herbie my iguana / making snow shapes on my carpet floor, so I'm not really across this. What do you think has changed in your body recently? Are you doing anything different?"*

Another response to "Do you think I've gained weight?" could be, *"I'm not sure. But, how do you feel lately? Are you feeling good? Or, feeling like something is different than usual?"* Shift the conversation from "how you look" to "how you feel. Asking the enquirer some leading questions will help open up the conversation and allow you to give more targeted feedback if necessary. A lot of times, this type of question is really asking for validation, that the enquirer is hoping that their body does not appear to the rest of the world as it does to them.

Another great question you can ask if someone asks if you think they've gained or lost weight is: *"What are some things you normally do to feel good? Walk? Meditate? Naps? Have you been doing those things lately, or not so much?"* This is helpful to see if any changes in their daily routine could account for changes in body shape. I'd also listen carefully to their responses if they mention health issues that might have accompanied weight gain/loss, as sometimes this can indicate a percolating problem. If something in their response indicated any kind of health-related issue, I'd advise the enquirer to get it checked out with their health professional likety-split.

If someone is insistent, "I need to lose weight!" you could respond by saying, *"Maybe instead of focusing on how much you weigh, you could focus on how you want to feel. Perhaps you want to feel alert, energetic, athletic, or confident, for example. What are some actions that would help you feel that way?"* This can help shift the conversation from weight to lifestyle and overall health.

※ ※ ※

I want to circle back to me, me, fabulous me. Since I pass judgement on my body every day, I reckon there's a fair to a high proportion of people reading this that are doing the same to their amazing and incredible bodies. I know I'm not going to stop judging my body and just accept it as is; that's a bridge too far for me. But I can choose to focus on the positive over the negative.

Such as:

"I know my thighs are not the size I want—but I'm pretty stoked about how powerful they are when I row."

"My stretch marks are visible beneath my bikini line—but so what? You have to be a hot lover to get an invite to see them up close."

"My breasts are small...good. Because I love to free to tit and go braless!"

"My upper arms are flabby. So what? They are excellent when it comes to hugs."

"I can't get rid of my bulging lower belly....but I can draw attention to my awesome shoulders!"

Next time you're cataloguing your own perceived body flaws, try to interrupt this pattern by mixing in some compliments and shout-outs for the only body you'll ever have. It's not kind or helpful to continually berate yourself for the body that you inhabit. Self-criticism is toxic and harmful. Give you and your body a break; you just might see the features, not the perceived flaws.

B IS ALSO FOR "THE BUSINESS"

Listen, I was in business before it was a thing that all the hideously overpaid CEOs, digital dude-bros, crypto-peddling charlatans, white wellness women warriors and the vacuous influencers turned into a "calling" that has disappeared up its own arse.

I've been in business so long it was called, you know, having a business and not being an entrepreneur. God, that word and how it's been co-opted to cover anything from your brother-in-law running a second-hand tyre business out of his cousin's backyard shed through to online course creators shilling hard their courses to other budding online course creators as the most audacious pyramid scheme ever...is enough to make you break shit.

To be clear, I'm all about personal determination and if your dream is to have a business, have at it, and I shall pray hard for you. But in all the puffery in being an "entrepreneur" and the trumpeting of making "6 and 7 figures" where you can work from anywhere, including shitty resorts in countries that are often under martial law, obscures the fact that having is business is hard fucking work that no one right in the head would take it on. Firstly, the paperwork and government regulations you need to operate under are enough to crush the hardiest souls. Knowing that you're responsible for the livelihoods of your team and having the cash flow to pay the relentless stream of tax bills keeps you rigid in bed with fear at night. And any fucker that tells you to "live in the now" has NEVER run a business as it's all about forward cash positioning and future workflow scheduling to know when to go hard in business development or pull back and maintain market share.

And yet...I find myself with a business entering its 22nd year.

The worst experience I've had as a business owner is making staff redundant due to changing business conditions. Fortunately, I had the support of a professional Human Relations consultant to guide me through the process. Still, without a doubt, it was the lowest point for me professionally, and I can only imagine how guttered the person who was redundant felt through the process. Apart from Human Relations consultants that can offer support and guidance through your legal obligations, there's a wealth of good advice on the internet to help you have this gut-wrenching conversation and navigate the tough time in the aftermath.

※ ※ ※

The things I found made a difference with being the person delivering the redundancy news were:

Make the time between the announcement of a meeting to discuss a business restructure and the actual meeting relatively short. No one wants to wait a week, knowing their future in the business is up in the air. That time hanging out in limbo-land is fraying everyone's nerves.

Try to do it in-person if possible. I know there's a pandemic still ranging, and parking is a bit, but this sort of news is delivered best in person as a sign of respect and professionalism.

Give yourself plenty of time on either side of the restructuring meeting to be calm. Have notes to refer to that map out the key information you need to give to the other person in the meeting (such as entitlements, the next steps etc.) and free yourself of other distractions so you can show up fully to the conversation and decompress on the other side.

Enlist a friend or business buddy to call both before and after the meeting to offer support and accountability that you're doing this shit thing, but you're not a rubbish person for having to make the hard and difficult business decisions.

During the meeting with the person being redundant, think about how you'd want to be treated and DO THAT. Be empathetic (*"I know this will be very difficult to her but we're no longer in a position to employ you"*) but don't make it about you and your pain ("I've been up all night crying about what I have to tell you"). Keep to the facts—such as a decline in business revenue—and don't go off tangent mentioning things like needing their car space back to help reduce business costs. Be honest with them if they have questions *"yes, your role was made redundant over Zoe, who has a similar position. In reviewing job descriptions, we realised that we had less of a need for your skillset in the next 12 months,"* but not too honest or unkind "We never really thought you fitted in, anyway!"

Keep the meeting brief and to the point. You don't need to spend hours rehashing the business history that led to this decision. But do offer the ability to have a follow-up meeting to answer any questions. The redundancy might have been suspected, but it's still a shock nonetheless.

And while it's helpful for you as a business owner or an employee of a firm that has to deliver news about redundancies to remind yourself that it's not personal, it's a business decision—it certainly feels very personal to the person who is made redundant. Be kind. Be honest and direct. You have a solemn responsibility to treat the person being made redundant with compassion and care as they have a massive blow to their confidence and will be experiencing uncertainty around finances and their future.

Offer any resources you can. This might look like work placement support, being a referee, or any connections or introductions you might have that will help them look for a new role.

And from one business owner to another—this biz shit is whitewater. Go gently with yourself, matey.

Avoid these clangers:

"I hate doing these redundancy meetings; everyone always cries". Honey...no.

Sending news of the redundancy via text. What—were you raised by hyenas?!?

"You'll have no trouble getting another job" You don't know that for sure, and while you think this would be comforting to hear, it hits differently for the person now faced with looking for new employment.

C IS FOR COMMITMENTS

You got those big arse style commitments like marrying and knocking out some ankle-biters. Then you have smaller everyday commitments like collecting said ankle-biters from the "Socrates 4 Kids" camp, making plans to get your hairdo done and volunteering for the local women's shelter. I put it to you that these smaller, daily commitments cause so much more grief than "Should I marry Trev?"

The daily knot twisting in the stomach over a pack-train of requests to organise a bake sale, have a knees-up with the ladies, swing the car around to pick up someone who shuns public transport and help out at the upcoming "Rehome a feral cat" luncheon. I mean, it's a full-time job fielding requests, deciding what you have time for. Then concluding that you need to work out a plan to stage your own death, so you don't have to deal with the sad panda face of someone let down by your inability to do ALL things requested of you.

Let's all agree that there will never be enough hours to do even a half-arsed job at fulfilling all the commitments asked of you. Well-deserving charities will forever need more hands to help those in need. Your loved ones will always pester you into showing up for their insufferable school concerts[5], and your friends will harass you into hanging out with them at an overpriced bar with a dubious vibe.

You got a life to live and shit to do; you do not have time to abandon your plans—even if that plan is to do fuck all on the Jason recliner—to fulfil all the commitments others pressure you to take on.

A friend of mine, who's a genius, has an email mailbox set up only for school, charities and other people classed as friends-by-association. The invites, and requests for assistance go straight to that box and bingo-bango, an automated message is spat out a day later saying, *"Thank you for your email. I'm not able to attend this event or help out. I hope it's a success!"* Genius, I tell you.

But that bit of higher consciousness thinking only works if requests are sent via email. Most are made in-person and when you are vulnerable to agreeing to anything. You're caught on the hop finishing your melting ice cream cone, hiding a wailing child in the station wagon or skulking home so you can kick off your pinching high heels. I mean, shit, I once sponsored a Kodiac Bear for 18 months as I was caught at a low point in life. The charity worker was very, very effective in their pitch. I saw that bear as an extension of my broken self, and OF COURSE, I needed to pay for nuts, berries and a warm den for that sad bear. I could only break that financial commitment after I got my life together and felt strong enough to call the Sad Bear Charity and turf that bear off my largesse so it could stop wallowing and embrace its best-bear life.

So yeah, the fuckers have caught you in a tight spot, asked you to commit, and now it's time to say these good things:

"I'm sorry, I'm not able to attend/help out", AND THEN SAY NO MORE. WELD YOUR TRAP SHUT. You don't owe anyone a total breakdown and full rebuttal—no is enough, lovers.

"I'll need to check my calendar. I'm pretty sure I have another commitment at that time" This is helpful when you hate saying no to a person face-to-face, and you'd prefer to send a text or email or make a call later. It's already set the scene that you're making an 80% "nope" deposit but just need some time to deliver the final 20% balance. But it's important you don't name your other commitment—you'll see why below.

"Sure, I can help out. As long as you're able to return the favour by helping me clean out my grease trap / the stall of my tea-cup pig / demolish my asbestos-riddled outhouse". This is some next-level Hannibal Lector quid pro quo shit. If someone asks something of you, here's your chance to rope a-dope and get them to pony up for you. Flick that funky "give freely of yourself without anything in return" homily. Massive shirkers who had zero intention of doing anything for other people except themselves coined that sort of righteous, smug insipidity. Or, in other words, the fundamentalist Christian Right.

Under no circumstances are you to say things like:

"If you have trouble getting someone, let me know, I'll help out then" Nawwww...all the enquirer heard was, *"Feel free to*

ask no one else and guilt me into doing this with another approach into 24 hours. I'll roll over like a rotisserie chicken."

"I mean, I'd really love to, but I have the kids that weekend / I don't really have anything to wear / I'm a progressive voter, and I'm not sure that the Qanon Gin and Pin night is for me". While you're introducing a soft no here—you've undone all your good work by naming your other commitment, and now you've opened the door of opportunity for the enquirer to pony up childcare, their glitter hot pants, their cousin Helena to convince you that Qanon is not the flogs you suspect them to be. Give no quarter readers, make like a spy when spying was cool and intriguing, and you wore trench coats and listened to Morse code with a headphone to one ear while you smoked silk cut cigarettes and offer no explanation!

"I'm a no for this request, but I'll be there for the next one!" Wha...no! The "next one" will be in approximately 3.5 days, and you'll be in this same position again, trying to beg off from another thing you don't want to do. You don't have to dress up your "No" or soften it. No is a baller. It can stand by itself. No buttressing is required.

D IS FOR DISASTERS, NATURAL STYLE!

In the spring/summer of 2019/2020, Australia endured the greatest loss of life, homes, bushland, farms, native wildlife and ecosystems in its white colonised history. Every state and territory shared in this devastation; even capital cities were not spared with fire threatening their outskirts and choking the air with toxic smoke and pollution. This dark, galling period is on track to be Australia's worst natural disaster, and it will take years, if not decades, for people to rebuild and for the bush and wildlife to regenerate.

I planned my 2019 New Years' Eve as a pretty tame event. Go to the movies to see the latest Star Wars movie instalment, eat ice cream and then go home and exfoliate. You need clean, scrubbed skin to see in the new year. Start as you mean to go on and all that.

Late in the afternoon of a tinder-dry New Year's Eve, my sister Emma called me. I was at home in Sydney, she was in Hawks Nest on holiday, and a fire had sprung up at Charmhaven, the neighbouring suburb where she had a home and where my parents had a home right next door to my sister. The day had been hideous, New South Wales was in extreme fire danger, and it was declared a state of emergency, so great was the fire risk. Emma had already called Mum and Dad to ask if they'd seen or heard anything about the fire, and the response was... "What fire?" Context: my mum and dad have both simple flip phones with no "Fires Near me" app. Couple that with the house shut tight to keep the scorching heat at bay; they were blissfully unaware of the fire marching towards them. I decided it was a good move for me to be with them at Blue Haven rather than an hour and a half away, so I chucked the basics (exfoliation mitt) in the car and drove up to see my parents.

When I arrived in Blue Haven, I drove to the ridgeline that looked out over Charmhaven. The fire was contained to the other side of the river. Black smoke billowed into the air. You could see flames climbing the tall trees. A chopper dropped water on top of the fire. I shared a video of the scene with my sister, and we both agreed that while things didn't look fab, it was on the other side of the river, and plenty of firefighters were working to contain it.

Back at my parent's place, the calm was broken by a low-flying jet dropping fire retardant on the Blue Have properties fronting the river. Mum and I shared potato chips for dinner while listening to the sombre ABC radio broadcasts giving updates on the multitudes of raging fires across the state. It seemed that everything was on fire. My phone buzzed with updates from Emma, who was on their local neighbourhood watch Facebook page with reports of where the fire was and the local roads that were being closed due to firefighting efforts.

And then all hell broke loose.

The fast-moving southerly that would usually offer respite from the heat blew strong and whipped up the fire, so it jumped the river and began the march up the hill towards the centre of Blue Haven. With the increased sound of sirens and the intensity of smoke now overhead, our phones lit up with the message it was time to either get out or enact the fire plan and stay and defend. I asked mum what their bushfire plan was.

"Let it all burn!" She said while throwing up her hands.

"Well...we don't want to be too premature..." Dad began cautiously.

I walked to the window, through the verticals back with a flourish and just pointed theatrically at the plumes of black smoke that had obliterated the setting sun and the helicopters that now hovered close overhead.

I called Emma and told her we were preparing to evacuate, and I asked what she wanted me to retrieve from her house. She wanted the much-loved toys on her daughter's beds that had been with them from birth and the ashes of her first Daushund, Maximus Decimus Maurillus Williamson the First.

I set Mum and Dad with the task while I retrieved those precious items from Emma: gather whatever items you need to evacuate and start loading the car. Dad still looked unsure about this urgency (FLAMES!!! FIRE!! WHAT EXACTLY IS THE POINT THAT YOU DO DECIDE TO MAKE MOVES??!?) while Mum sat resolutely in her walker with her meds and her embroidery on her lap. Huh. Guess she was serious about letting it all burn to the ground.

I jogged next door to my sister's place, and as I was fumbling with keys, I was met by Mavis, their elderly neighbour from across the road. Mavis was unsure what to do. She got an emergency services text message, but what did it all mean? I stopped arguing with the door and faced Mavis.

"Mavis, it means that we have to get ready to go. The fire is nearby, and it's not safe to stay. Have you got your stuff that you want to evacuate with?"

"Well, no...what would I even take?"

"As a start, I'd suggest your medication, any documents like medical scripts, bank statements, some water, snacks and a change of clothes and toiletries. Any anything that holds personal significance for you."

"Oh!" Mavis said brightly. "I need to take my mother's china cabinet."

With an eye on the reddening horizon and the sound of the wind lashing the smoke and flames about, I knew I had to move this along. "No, Mavis, only stuff that can fit in your car. I've got to get Emma's stuff now. How about you gather your things, and I'll come across as soon as I've put this in the car?"

I darted through Emma's dark, quiet house, collected her things, including her laptop and computer, and locked the house hurriedly. As I'm packing that stuff into my car, I hear a voice, "Excuse me...are you from the fire brigade?" Reader...I am clad in my activewear, and it is troubling to me that someone should mistake someone in activewear really doing nothing that would warrant the wearing of activewear...for a member of the professional firefighting contingent.

"No... I'm Fiona, Noelene and Graeme's daughter...are you ok?"

The elderly woman balanced uncertainly on a walking stick. "No... I'm having a panic attack. I'm so worried about the fires and my dogs. I'm Helen," she said tearfully.

"Ok," I said with my niece's peter rabbit stuffed doll under one arm and the ashes of my nephew's dachshund under the other. "How about we breathe together. Let's breathe in for three and out for five. Can you do that with me?

We stand in the street, breathing together as the street empties of cars. A car passes behind Helen. "That's my husband; he's going to see what's going on".

"Not a smart move", I mutter to myself, and I return my focus to Helen, whose anxiety is lessening. "How about you get your stuff that you need to evacuate, and I'll come back to check on you in a sec?"

"You won't leave without me?" She asks worriedly.

I look her square in the eye, "I promise I won't go without you".

"I need to get my six dogs ready too…"

I'd been wondering about the cacophony in the house behind her. Perfect. I now had six dogs to wrangle into my hatchback if her useless husband didn't return from his ill-advised reconnaissance mission.

"We'll take them too!" I announced confidently.

I jogged back to the car, placed in the last of Emma's precious haul and remembered that Dawn, Emma's other elderly neighbour, might not be with her family this New Year's Eve, and it's worth checking in on her. With the red glow getting ever closer and the Fire's Near Me app showing the fire eight streets away, I break into a run. As I sprint past Mavis's place, her husband Dennis reverses the car out. With the passenger doors open. I yell out to try and alert him…but the doors scrape the sides off the garage opening as he can't hear me over the Kenny Rogers country mix he has blasting on the car stereo. Yeah...of course, every disaster should have a Kenny Rogers soundtrack to it. Deciding I can't do anything now to prevent the collision, I jog onto Dawn's house.

I knock on Dawn's door and hear her shuffling towards it.

"Dawn... it's Fiona, Noelene and Graham's daughter. Can you open up, please?"

She opens the door, holding Trixie, her old scruffy dog, in her arms.

"Are you here about the fire?" She asks me.

"Yes, Dawn, it's time we got stuff ready to go."

"I thought about calling my son...but I didn't want to worry him."

"That's ok, Dawn, we will all go together. Do you need a hand packing the car and getting it out of the garage?"

She looks at the three hessian shopping bags in the hallway. "No, I have everything ready". She looks at me as she pats a shaking Trixie. "I'm really scared."

"I am too, Dawn", and for a moment, all the activity stops, and we look at each other with the acknowledgement of what we're both truly feeling and the uncertainty of what's to come throughout the night. It's the first time that day I'm in the moment and not running disaster scenarios and packing lists through my head. I'm scared, and I don't know how this will play out.

We got lucky that night. Through the intense and ballbusting efforts of the firefighters, only garden sheds and lawn lockers were lost in Blue Haven. Everyone remained safe, and no loss of human life occurred. But the devastation of the natural bushland was ghastly, and so many animals and birds were either dead, injured or without their bush homes.

I think back to that night, and I'm glad I took a moment in the maelstrom to share how I was feeling with Dawn. That I didn't try and jolly along with a grown-ass woman with false platitudes like "it's going to be fiiiiine!" Because the truth was, I didn't know how the night would turn out. So many people in the summer of fire had gone through what we had with devastating outcomes that ended with death and destruction. As I said, we got damn, fucking lucky when so many others didn't.

Look, there's no shortage of natural disasters to try out these good words to say, ESPECIALLY if you're Australian.

"The whole event sounds so ghastly. How are you doing?" It's natural for our curiosity to want to know how close the fire got and how much stuff was lost in the floods. But all of that is immaterial—how is your person doing? A tiredness settles in your bones, dealing with the aftermath of a natural disaster. Please focus less on the sensational or lurid aspects of the disaster can keep your attention on the human behind the headlines.

"I know you're probably assessing what you need in the way of help with so many offers. But I'm committed to helping out long term, so I'll be checking in each fortnight to see what

might have come up as an urgent need". This is really helpful to the person who's been through the disaster. The initial in-flood of support, assistance and tangible items wanes over time, so it's good for those affected to hear that you're in their corner for the long haul and when to expect your check-ins. People who've lost so much in a disaster can find it terribly challenging to their sense of pride to ask for help, so take that burden from them and be the one to make the call and offer what support you can.

"I'm available for the cleanup, and I can bring supplies. Is 9 am on Tuesday good for you?" Most disasters have a heavy component of cleaning up and making good. It's tedious and tiring work, especially for the person who has lost so much. If you can, please volunteer for clean up/make good duties. Wear good, strong and comfortable footwear. Depending on the conditions, dress in layers that can be shed or added to. Bring water, snacks, sunblock, hand sanitiser, a quality dusk mask, sturdy gloves and insect repellant. The pungent smells from rotting food and the entire home submerged underwater are like no other. Try for some good ol' Vicks or essential oils just under the nostrils to block out the odours. And bring a first aid kit to dress any wounds you might end up with from removing debris. You should treat any wound or skin puncture immediately to prevent infection and sickness.

※ ※ ※

Let's make a pact to avoid bullshit like this:

"At least you're ok. You can replace other things." I've been guilty of saying this, and I really wish I could take it back.

For someone who has lost everything except for the clothes they're standing in, being alive and facing the enormity of replacing everything from a fridge to a facial scrub is extremely burdensome. Add to that the loss of so many treasured keepsakes and irreplaceable items. It can seem like being alive is some sort of cruel second-prize draw.

"Well, insurance should cover most of the replacement costs. It's all just stuff anyway" When I asked my sister what she wanted me to collect from her home as the fire raced toward it, there was a pause as she mentally ran through the things precious to her that make a home. Her wedding dress, the photo albums of happy family times, the cross stitches she's done for her daughters that hand with pride in their rooms, the hand-made patchwork quilts our mum made, the jeans that fit just right, the handbag that she bought with her first pay-check, the hand-made jewellery her daughters have made her...give it to me one more time that this is all just easily replaceable "stuff".

"You knew you were building in a fire/flood/earthquake zone. What did you expect?" This sort of rationalisation is breathtakingly ignorant. Many cheap tracts of land are susceptible to natural disasters, and because of that, some people who might not otherwise be able to afford to live in areas not so likely to endure the threat of floods and fire live on these lands. They weigh up the risk of cheaper land against the threat of a 1 in a 100-year flood and drought zone and decide to play the odds. Also, many areas once deemed safe have also become flood and fire zones because of climate change. This is a threat we need to deal with as a community and not blame people whose only option for a home of their own was on uninsurable lands.

D IS ALSO FOR DIVORCE AND BREAKUPS

I got from here. I spent much of my 20s through to late 40s casually dating, interspersed with some longer-term relationships. While I've never married or divorced, I know the breakup badlands very well.

A particularly memorable breakup occurred when someone dumped me via text. Nothing to see here, I hear you say. That's common enough on most Tuesdays.

Except:

I'd dated him for a year, enough time to form emotional bonds and believe you were worth more than a 50-word text advising you were no longer dating.

He got married to another woman who I'd never heard of in another town only six months later. Cool, cool, except there was no discussion about us being anything but monogamous when we were dating.

He then undertook PhD study into what it means to be a "Good Bloke".

WOW. Ok. The self-delusion in that one is strong.

So straight out of the gate, please—for the love of all things sandwiches—if you have someone in your circle going through a divorce or breakup, don't say, "Oh, I'm sorry to hear you broke up with them". Pause. Insert sad face. Then brightly: "No matter, another partner is just around the corner".

This advice is excellent for buses. Most likely, there is another one around the next corner. It's rather fucked advice if you're after a partner, through. There's no guarantee that another is leaving the depot bound for your stop anytime soon.

※ ※ ※

Approach sidebar if you're coupled or thriced up[6]: You are shit at advising on breakups. I don't want to offend, but your semi-permanent state of being smug because you've got a plus one and are off the apps makes you exceedingly bad at saying something helpful when confronted by a break-up. It doesn't matter that you've suffered epically fraught breakups in the past. Your current state of coupledom means you're willfully blind to another's breakup pain and will say rubbish things like:

"I never liked Maurice anyway. He always smelt of blue cheese and spoke of himself in the third person". Steer clear of these lovers, like Lazarus rising. As soon as you've trashed the ex, they'll be back on the scene with flowers, scented lube and promises not to sext the intern.

"That's a shame you divorced Shanae...still, I always wondered if you'd wise up after you caught them giving blow jobs during the team building sessions". You might have receipts

on the past partner, but it doesn't mean that your friend is caught up on this news or is in a position to hear all about their previously hidden sexual talents.

"I'm so glad you divorced Holly. I've been meaning to tell you that I've always had a thing for you". This might play well in the rom-com starring Meg Ryan, but it lands like a piece of lead when you bust it out in real life. First up, someone grieving the end of a relationship might like a hot minute before thinking about dating and mating. Next up, carrying a torch for someone for an extended period of time without doing a damn thing about it is not exactly marking you as a go-getter. More likely a buzzard that's waiting for the opportune moment to pick over the carcass of a dead relationship.

Some helpful things you could say:

"Breakups are THE WORST. I'm shocked at this news. I'm coming around with cake and tea. What else can I pick you up on the way" It's tempting to isolate yourself when you are in the shockwaves of a separation. Please be that person who keeps in regular contact and drops in so they know they don't have to white-knuckle their way through the pain.

"I know you're in a lot of pain right now. Can I take one thing off your plate to help out?" Asking for "one thing" is a lot less daunting than saying "let me know if I can be of help", as the shopping list of stuff they are dealing with is lengthy. It might run from the minutiae of separating your car registration from the shared toll account to the big shifts where you

need to find a new place to live or negotiate shared care of the kids. Removing one thing off that list is an act of love.

"I know this might be confronting so lose to the breakup, but I want to check in that you have got your own bank account or access to your cash" When I broke up with my fiancé, a posse of my girlfriends rocked up with groceries, wine, flowers and very good advice. And that advice was secure your cash. Make sure that you extract your share of funds from any joint account. Money means choices, and too many (women especially) are shell-shocked from a breakup and don't sure up the cash before it's too late. Please remind your person to do this and get what's theirs.

E IS FOR "EH...WAIT... WHAT?!?!"

I sometimes consult the tarot. Upon waking, I pull a card and reflect: "What sort of fuckery is about to greet me when I step foot outside my pad?" I like to be forewarned about big, incoming news as I can't guarantee that my face and words will form good and helpful sentences and that I won't resort to "WHAT THE TITS IS THIS?!?" Which is usually not helpful. At all.

Apparently, others have some trouble coping with BIG NEWS too.

A friend's parents pretended not to hear when their daughter Rey came out to them over a Sunday lunch. The "sorry, didn't catch that" continued through dessert, the dishes, the small talk over the cricket on the Telly, the folding of the washing and the wave goodbye at the end of the day. In fact, the denial dragged on until Rey, some 18 months later after the initial coming out, decided the problem was the volume, not the message and yelled, "I'M GAY, I'M GAY, I'M GAY, I'M GAY, I'M GAY" while standing at the counter of her parents news-agency during the rush for morning bus tickets, newspapers and scratch lottery cards.

Another friend Bronwyn worked up tremendous courage to

tell her elderly parent Barb that she was breaking up with her shitbag of a husband, Ted. Barb had always loved Ted and Bronwyn knew the news would hit hard, so she'd compiled a neatly written list in her daily diary about what Ted was an arse of a husband and rubbish human being. Bronwyn finished telling Barb, closed her diary and placed it carefully in her handbag, smoothed her skirt and waited for Barb to say something. The clock on the sideboard ticked over. Bronwyn cleared her throat. The sound of the heating thermostat clicked on. Bronwyn shifted on her chair and tried to catch Barb's eye; the suspense was maddening. Unable to endure another moment, Bronwyn reached over and patted her mother's cardigan-clad arm.

"Mum...I wondered what you thought about what I said... about Ted?"

Barb jolted upright, startled and furiously jabbed at her hearing aid.

"What...WHAT...sorry, love, I must have had the hearing aid off! Damn nuisance it is...now, what was that?"

Linda had been dating Michael for 18 months, and they were enraptured with each other. Discovering she was unexpectedly pregnant, Linda booked a night at an expensive hotel to break the happy news to Michael that they were to be parents.

Over a swoon-worthy dinner with candles, delicious food and first-class service, Linda leaned in, held Michael's hand and said, "Honey, I've got some fabulous news... we're having a baby!" Tears glistened in Linda's eyes, and she choked back happy sobs.

Michael was stunned: "Are you sure it's mine?!?!"

Vee's 22-year marriage to Chris had run its course, and they decided to separate. The breaking apart was done with care, grace and minimal angst. The love between them had diluted, and they were more friends than lovers and life partners. One day, the neighbour and long-time friend Sienna caught Vanessa home after Chris had moved out.

"Vanessa....I....I.....I had to tell you that I had always loved you, and I was hoping we could explore our relationship together."

"Ah yes...." Vanessa began cautiously, not entirely sure what was being said here.

"Like as in friends? Going out more...as friends?" She said hopefully.

"No, Like I want to kiss you and have you as my girlfriend" Sienna clarified.

"Ehhhhhhhh......" And Vanessa drooped the vase she was holding, marking that as an exclamation mark to the entire conversation.

...And I'm sure you can add your own "Wait...What?" Story to this list. It's pretty much guaranteed that the moment you're:

- In the middle of lathering up your hair real good with shampoo
- Holding something breakable and most likely a family heirloom
- In the biggest rush of all time, with your hair on fire
- Busting to have a pee
- ABSOLUTELY on your last nerve

The absolute banger of a song comes on that is TOTALLY your jam

...BIG NEWS is about to drop.

Apart from the tarot that is the spiritual version of the budgie in the coal mine, I have found it helpful to deploy this little phrase when I'm nose to nose with BIG NEWS.

"Can you tell me a little more about that?"

Yes. It's counterintuitive. It's not what you really mean in the moment. It's the opposite of what you really want to say, which is "WHAT THE EVER LIVING FUCK?!?!" But this handy little phrase will buy you precious time to rearrange your brain and form proper and helpful words in your mouth while the person with BIG NEWS expands on their BIG NEWS.

※ ※ ※

Let's take it for a test drive, shall we?

Call: "Mum...Dad, I'm gay." / Response: *"Ok...can you tell me a little more about this?"*

Call: "Barb, Ted has been banging his intern, and I'm leaving his saggy arse." / Response: *"This is indeed shocking information...can you tell me more about it."*

Call: "Vanessa, I want to sex you up Colour Me Badd style, even though you're fresh out of your break up with your husband."

/ Response: *"Can you tell me a little more about that but in the meantime, please release my breast from your grasp?"*

Works a treat, doesn't it? It's such a genius phrase as it gives the BIG NEWS some room to breathe and for everyone to take a hot minute and collect themselves.

Usually, the person with the BIG NEWS they have been holding this in for some time, ruminating on it and imagining how it will land. So BIG NEWS usually get blurted out and "can you tell me a little more about it" acts as a hand brake as the new information ripples out into the open space.

I gave this phrase a red hot go with a friend Sally. Sally's mum who had been absent from the family for many years, had surfaced, and she wanted to see her daughters and explain why she had walked out on the family when Sally was only a small child. The timing of the talk coincided with our long-planned annual girls' weekend away. Sally was distraught when she told me about this on the phone. Between ugly crying and trying to share the story of her mum's reappearance with repeated sorry's…it was a lot for Sally to share. I listened and waited until there was a break in the "I'm so sorry / I've stuffed all of our plans" and said softly, "Sally, can you tell me a bit more about how you're really doing with having your mum re-enter your life".

With a direct question that focused on only one of the things Sally was juggling, it calmed her, and she explained how unexpected this approach by her mum was and how conflicted she felt.

One of the greatest gifts we can give is the opportunity to be heard and really listened to. If you're a fan of Fleabag, AND YOU SHOULD BE, the writer and lead actress Phoebe Waller-Bridge was asked about the enduring appeal of her love interest in the second series Hot Priest. Her take on it is that his hotness is directly related to how he listens and really listens to her character. He's interested in what she says, and he does not shrink from her pain or contradictions. Oh, to be really, really seen and heard, isn't that the ultimate? No one seeking to fix us, talk over us, tell us via a meandering tale of how they faced something similar, but it wasn't something similar it was a story that pulled the focus back to them, and now you're deflated, promising yourself you'll be careful opening your heart to another's in the future.

In times when isolation and loneliness are rising like a tide despite all the connectivity promised by social apps, give the priceless gift of your attention and non-judgement of, *"Can you tell me a little more about that?"*

Enquiring minds want to know! Here are some other questions to open up the dialogue, buy you some time to collect your thoughts and not blurt out something that marks you as a dick and added bonus—will put you in the realm of Hot Priest:

"How did that make you feel?" A good line of enquiry for stalling so you can think of an appropriate and caring next question.

"I can see/hear that sharing this news is important to you... is this something you've been thinking about for a while?" The acknowledgment of the BIG NEWS is important to the person delivering it, even though it might be trifling to you. Validate that shit!

"So, what do you think will be your next move?" This is helpful

as the answer will give you clues in ways that you can be further support to them

"Are you safe?" Some BIG NEWS is delivered in dire circumstances such as domesticated violence, accidents, natural disasters and general traumatic situations. First things first... is the person safe, and if not, how can you help them get to a place of safety?

"What help or support can I offer you going forward?" Another excellent question. You don't just want to hear BIG NEWS and then beg off to go tend to your bonsai. No, be a good human and be there for your person.

"Have you told anyone else about this?" Not an obvious choice but helpful in establishing if there might be others that can come together as a support network to help this person during this difficult time.

"Thank you for telling me". I just have to turn off the stove/pullover/step out of work so I can listen to you with zero interruptions. I'm going to call you straight back in 10, is that ok? Sometimes BIG NEWS is going to come at you in the most inopportune time. Get to a place where you can listen to your person without distraction and get back on that call.

BIG NEWS should not be met with:

"Do we have to do this right now? There's a show on the TV, and it might never be shown again." Who gives a fuck, Susan?

Switch off the goddamn TV! You can catch it on the recaps. Be like the Hot Priest and listen up good and proper.

"I'm not sure I'm the one you should be telling this to." Neither am I numb-nuts, but for some reason, someone sees a compassionate and caring person in the shape of you, so honour that.

"Oh, I've known about this for ages." Good for you, Sherlock, but your friend might have just realised they were gay, their partner was cheating on them or that Lizzo is the one true religion. So park your smugness and listen with kindness.

"If you think that's bad, let me tell you about the time I had a cyst on my lady parts". Honey...no.

"Wait a minute. I'm just going to get a bottle of wine / a line of coke / some meth so I can take this in." Not the time for checking out with substances as it heightens the chance of saying something unhelpful or just passing out. Turn off Cypress Hill, put down the bong and be as clear-headed as you can to hear BIG NEWS so you can support me in all the best ways I know you're capable of.

"Wait till I tell Jane about this!" You're telling no one anything about this conversation, got it? Even with permission from the person with BIG NEWS, it's not yours to share. Be as silent as the grave and zip it.

"Is that it? Is that the BIG NEWS?" Look, someone's six-inch is someone's twelve-inch, and I'm not just talking Subway sandwiches here. Just because it's no big deal to you doesn't mean it isn't life-altering, earth-quaking news to another. Treat BIG NEWS with respect and brevity. If it means something to your person, it means equally the same for you.

F IS FOR FRIENDS

I subscribe to the view that blood relatives are the family we get, but friends are the family we choose. And sometimes, like eating cheese out of a spray can, those choices are not in our best interests. Friends are great—until they aren't. My Grandad was staunch on this point: a friend in need is a pain in the arse.

And please don't get it twisted; sometimes, WE are the actual pain in the arse. I've been a good friend and a bad friend. The times I've been a bad friend still make me wince as we'd all like to be known as that dependable, thoughtful and cherished friend. I know I've failed to live up to this standard many, many times.

I've forgotten the birthdays and milestone dates of my closest friends.

I've taken a pass on attending celebrations and get-togethers for the flimsiest of reasons.

I've opted for the temporary comfort of a lie over the truth that I know will bite hard.

I haven't checked in when I said I would or haven't maintained contact as closely as I should have when friends are going through challenging times.

I've been all that and more, and I continue to want to do better even though I miss the mark occasionally. Knowing we've let down a friend is a special sort of ache. We'd all like to describe ourselves as good mates, but when we know we're failing to meet minimum standards, we're ashamed and can retreat further from the friendship, causing further erosion.

My friend Olivia, who's married, once had an affair with a man who also worked at the same place she did. Her husband had limited interest in sex and intimacy, and Olivia was a raging furnace of hot desirability. The marriage had become more of friends than sexual partners, and Olivia desperately missed being touched and desired. Over the course of a number of slow-burn months, the attraction to her co-worker grew, and soon they became lovers, with the husband having no knowledge of this relationship beyond believing they were co-workers that got along amicably.

Olivia confided in me about this relationship, and reader, I was a shitty friend. I really liked Olivia's husband. He was an articulate, funny and engaging company, so I had a vested interest in their partnership. When Olivia told me about the affair, I was shocked. I said a few meaningless things like, "well, as long as you know what you're doing," and I rushed to change the subject as I was already in the full-blown judgement of Olivia. It took me many months to wake the fuck up and be a friend, not a judge of Olivia. I told her, "I'm sorry I didn't fully appreciate at the time what you were sharing with me, and I brushed you off. What I believe you were telling me, and that I should have focused on, was that you were unhappy in your marriage. Are you open to talking about this further with me?"

I'd rated Olivia's morals against my own, judged her harshly, and dipped out on the conversation and being a friend to her. By retreating from the dialogue and an opportunity to understand Olivia and the pain she was experiencing, I created a separation between us.

I'm lucky that Olivia accepted my apology. Since that time, I hope I've been more mindful of where judgement shows up for me and how being "the good girl" can be corrosive to the nuances of relationships in particular. Through Olivia's experience, I've understood how complex relationships are—especially sexual ones—and what might be great for one person can grind for another.

Some useful words for you when it comes to friendships:

"I'm sorry I can't make that dinner/celebration/event, but I'm not feeling my sparkly best at the moment. Is there another time that we can celebrate together, just the two of us?" I wish I'd said this personally to a number of friends when I was in the full-blown state of an anxiety attack or stuck in my introvert crypt rather than the last-minute impersonal text to say I couldn't make it. Not cool or kind to my friend when they rightfully had their knees up to mark an important occasion. A BIG regret of mine.

"From what you're describing to me, this sounds like an abusive relationship. Would you categorise it in the same way? Can I provide some immediate help?" Oh, I REALLY wish I'd said this when a friend B had laid out the past six months of

her relationship with her fiancé. Instead, I told her straight out to leave him. That was like going to DEFCON 1 in a flat three seconds. B was not at the stage of packing her belongings and moving out. She'd just taken the tentative steps to tell me of her partner berating her for how she'd spend joint finances and going missing for days on end after an alcoholic bender with his mates. She didn't need me to go nuclear on her. She needed a friend to be empathetic, hear her out and take the next step with her.

"I know I've been missing in action in recent times, and I'd like the chance to tell you more about why there's been radio silence. I miss you and your friendship. Can we make a time to catch up?" Life can pull us in all sorts of directions, and once-important relationships can slide into the background. If you want to reconnect, be prepared to own your part in not maintaining contact and make it a priority to stay in touch, even if it is with texts between calls or face-to-face meetups.

※ ※ ※

Friends don't let other friends say things like:

"I'm vaccinated, and you're not, so...we can't hang out". I'm pro-vac all the way. I'm so grateful that science and an excellent universal health care system (USA—you might want to get onto this) allowed us a path out of Covid and prevented so many unnecessary deaths. Having said that, there are many reasons why some people did not get vaccinated. But you won't know what those reasons are—the good and unhinged—if it's a blanket ban on friends whose views are not aligned with yours. I'll happily admit that it would be easier

to avoid all contact with friends who have wildly different beliefs from your own. But that's a cop-out. I should be willing to defend my views whilst also hearing another's position. The world is increasingly becoming divided along ideological lines, and we can't hope to reach across that divide without finding commonality. People are so much more than their views on a topic, and especially with friends, it's definitely worth the investment to understand another point of view. In this case, if a friend is vaccinated and the other isn't, it might mean that you catch up via a call or video conference. It does not mean that the friendship needs to cease, especially if there are any other issues you're aligned on and you share similar values. Of course, this advice is voided if they are barking mad and believe that Covid is all part of some nefarious plot by the governments to control the populace. I mean, have you ever tried to get a name change on a government database? If this takes three goes, several different forms to a number of government agencies, setting up a pin and password and then starting over because the app was in a beta phase....what's the actual likelihood of them also trying to gain absolute and total control over the people? Fucking two-fifths of bugger all, I reckon.

"I never thought you'd do something like that. I thought I knew you". Ah, but how well do we know anyone, even ourselves? Maybe a little less judgement and a little more seeking to understand the behaviour of your friend that's so confusing to you.

F IS ALSO FOR FREAKOUTS

The coolest cats will face freakouts many times in their life; it's just rare that you'll be around to witness it. So if you're the nervy type like me, please don't think that it's only you that has your equilibrium shaken up by unexpected events.

Back in 2018, I went through a shatter point. The way I'd been living my life was no longer sustainable, and I had a breakdown, even planning to end my own life. At that low point, I made a better choice to call the Suicide Prevention phone line and reach out to a dear friend who was in the same city I was visiting. While I no longer have suicide ideation, I do experience panic attacks that are like a hangover from past me wanting to harm myself. It's like there's part of my brain that's on permanent watch, making sure that anything considered slightly dangerous—driving at speed, riding a bike in an urban area where most drivers consider cyclists pests and on par with telemarketers—tips over into hyper-vigilance and then blooms into a full panic attack. It's a vibe killer when you have the tunes loaded, the snacks ready, and you're about to feel the freedom of cruising the highway and BOOM! You're in the grip of a panic attack, palms bathed in sweat, your breathing rapid and shallow, and your heart pounding like an EDM nightclub banger. It's a horrid experience, and apparently, it's not uncommon. What's working for me is exposure therapy, where I drive at a speed that I feel safe at (about 10 – 15kms) below the highway top speed and practising self-compassion.

※ ※ ※

If you're experiencing panic attacks, I'm going to suggest that I've also found helpful as the panic attacks have lessened in severity over the years:

"You're so brave trying to find a way through these panic attacks. Keep going".

"It might feel like you're going to die or pass out, but you won't. You've done this before, and you know the feeling passes".

"It won't be like this forever, even though it feels like it. You're moving through it, and each time you try, you're getting closer to the end of this".

Mostly though, I'd say to trust what you're experiencing. Many people have endured panic attacks, but not enough people are talking about it and what causes the attack to be triggered. Panic attacks fester in the dark, so if you share with others what you're going through, they can support and care for you. They'll also be your cheer squad as you keep marching forward to meet the panic attack with steely-eyed determination to overcome it.

※ ※ ※

I've also heard these helpful things from other peeps:

From the gorgeous and talented yogi Leah Simmons, founder of the mind, spirit, emotional, and body integrated program KAAIA, *"You can do this, you ARE doing this"*.

From my smart and compassionate Dr Melanie, *"Is there something in this experience that my subconscious wants to let me know?"* For me, my subconscious wants to make sure that I keep myself safe, even if it has become so overprotective the benign and everyday tasks of driving at speed can now trigger a panic attack. These attacks have also reminded me that it's ok to slow down and enjoy life in the slow lane rather than hurtle down the highway, tailgating others and generally being a menace on the roads.

From my man-friend G, *"You love driving and riding your bike too much. Don't give up. This challenge is worth overcoming"*. Naturally, seek advice from a trusted professional, but it's been helpful for me to continue to practise driving on highways and riding my bike. The safety of others is paramount, and I know what I need to do to keep them safe (drive at a speed I know that doesn't trigger an attack, notice the signs of an attack brewing and divert my brain before the attack overcomes me). But G is right; panic attacks and freaking out is worthy of overcoming. So I take some deep breaths, crank some Amyl and the Sniffers and cruise on up the highway.

✹ ✹ ✹

If you have a person in your life who experiences panic attacks but comments like these on ice:

"It's all in your head". Thanks for that, Scoop. This tea towel is, however, in my hands and about to give you a thwack across the back of the knees for an insensitive comment.

"Aren't you over this by now?" Panic attacks are slippery characters. You can be trucking along just fine, and then one will sideswipe you and then haunt your next few months before disappearing again. They don't work to any sort of timetable or an agreed set of conditions, much like State-run public transport. Fun, eh?

G IS FOR GIVING

The spirit of giving by either a financial donation or your time and effort is hard-baked into most of us. At the first sign of need, we contribute money to efforts on the ground, donate spare food and warm clothing and blankets to comfort those displaced and give up personal time so we can render assistance to those facing disaster and homelessness.

It gets fraught when you are continually tapped for more donations or time to help out. So we're clear, no matter how much time and money you're able to donate, you'll never cure all society's ills or save every person. Life can be cruel and unfair, and some people seem to have to endure the worst of life over and over. Humans are hard-wired to help each other—a trait curiously missing from most of the Trump and Putin sycophants—and there'll be times when you will have to say no to requests for help because you've maxed out your giving budget; you're already stretched for time or perhaps you need some help to get through a tough period.

Being unable to help another brings up so many awful feelings—guilt, especially. I know I'm still beating myself up over not helping others when I was at a low point and didn't have the courage to share that I, too, was struggling. I had been guilted to volunteer at an event at my Rowing Club when

I could barely leave the house without waves of panic washing over me. I turned up, gritted my teeth through the event, taking every opportunity to retreat to the change rooms, where I locked myself in a shower stall and braced myself against the tiled walls, just counting breaths until the anxiety passed. Pushing myself beyond what was fair and reasonable was not smart, and I spent the next week recovering, where I oscillated between bed and lounge, trying to revive my spirit.

Part of the human contract is the unspoken agreement that we help others in need without any thought of payback or even expectation to be thanked.

But what happens when you're tapped out, and you need to take a pass on a request?

You can keep it simple *"I'm sorry, but I'm not able to help at this time."* These are good words to say as it's succinct, and you don't have to catalogue the list of reasons why it's not possible for you to help out.

"I've reached the limit of my allotted donations for the month/year, but I'll keep this Charity/cause/person in mind when my budget resets". Only deploy this if it's true for you; otherwise, you're giving false hope and setting yourself up for another request for assistance when the time period you've mentioned comes due.

*"I'm not available that weekend when the working B / lamington drive / Punks for Peace is being held, but I'd be happy to

contribute $X dollars/order two dozen lamingtons / make a protest banner from tartan picnic blanket and safety pins instead". This is a clever response as it allows you to define how you'd like to be involved in the cause without feeling overtaxed or railroaded into something that you don't want to do.

※ ※ ※

Avoid saying:

"For sure! Happy to help any way I can". This response will trigger an avalanche of requests, and soon you'll be working all the hours god sends to ensure that the displaced Polar Bears are being billeted out amongst your mates, petitioning The Hague to recognise Polar Bears as true sovereign beings and you're bailing up unsuspecting types at the Cheese counter to ask them to buy "I'm a Polar Bear Pal" charity kerchief. Please do not open the floodgates and go all-in on the people-pleasing. Clearly define what you're prepared to do—and what you're not.

"Ohhhhhh…I would have donated to this, but last week I donated plasma and then on Tuesday night I hung out the Socialists Supper and then next week I've got the craft circle where we turn used printer cartridges into wearable art". Look, we're all doing what we can. We just don't need to hear about the myriad of ways you're a better human than me.

"I never give to charities; the money doesn't go to those in need" It's true that not every dollar you donate goes directly into the pocket of those I need. Charities have overheads to pay that include wages, entitlements, rents, insurance,

telecommunications and marketing. Some charities are better than others in getting more money for those in need. But a few less-than-prudent charities is no reason to snap your coin purse shut. Don't be the person that other people talk of and begin sentences with "Guess what that tight-arse is up to now...."

But lo, what if you're the person having to rally the troops to come forth and help out? What words can you say to inspire people to donate when you struggle to ask for help for yourself?

The first thing is not to make the request personally. While what you're asking for help for might benefit you in some way—for example, provide you with emergency accommodation during the loss of your home during a natural disaster or something with lower stakes like benefiting from a well presented Community Centre due to a fresh coat of paint and repairing the roof leaks—your ask usually helps more than one person so focus on the community that will benefit from your ask.

※ ※ ※

Good things to say to get a yes rather than them having to say they need to wash the cat:

"Hey, on Thursday afternoon, we're having a sit-in for 2 hours in the market square to bring awareness to the lack of social housing in the area. I know this issue is close to your heart. Can I count on you to be there?" I like this as it's a very defined request, including an expected time commitment

that's helpful for people to know if they can fit this in their calendar. It's also clever as it's targeting people that are passionate about the cause. This is preferable to be roped into donating time/energy/money into a cause that you could give a fuck about—like the raising of funds for a Trump-owned social shouty media platform for fascists and fuckheads that you just know is going to be stacked full of raging homophobes, racists and window lickers.

"I'm raising funds for Koala Bears. The money we raise will buy new tracts of land that will remain development free, so the koalas can live happily in their trees without being bulldozed". Also good as it's painting a picture of what the money will be specifically used for—not some vague collection scheme that has people scratching their heads over what the money will actually be used for.

"I found this great website to help support the Ukrainian people access money for home repairs due to shelling and also for basic needs. Can I send it to you?" This is helpful as you're spreading the word of how people are in need of help, but you're also allowing the person permission to send them the link before going off and bombarding them with daily emails cataloguing the horror that Ukrainians are living through. You're also providing them with a chance to look into the cause and decide if it's a right fit for them instead of being up their grill asking for an immediate donation.

H IS FOR HAIRY SITUATIONS

I'm a female working in the very male-dominated area of construction. I'm 50 now, and I got my start in the industry when I was 23, so while things for women have improved, there is still an enclave of men who believe a woman's place is anywhere but wearing a safety vest and steel caps.

I've tried to be understanding and sympathetic to their delicate sensibilities being undermined by the very reasonable request to remove the stack of copy paper from the women's toilets because I need to pee and just have a hot minute to myself. I've tried to see it from their point of view. I understand it's challenging coping with workplace cultural changes when it's been so comfortable and cosy having men dominate leadership roles. It must be tough to take direction from a woman when most interactions with women were via the tits out on pin-up wall calendars. I've been accommodating and encouraging...but fuck off to all that. There's been more than enough time for these dinosaurs to be grown arse adults and just get on board the change train.

When I was new to the industry, I went to a tile warehouse after work one evening to select floor tiles for an interior design project I was working on. Slowly walking through the stacks of ceramics, with the owner by my side offering the odd comment:

"From Italy. The very best."

"$29 per meter laid, you won't do better."

"Non-slip, perfect for the bathroom."

"Salmon. The most wanted colour right now". (It was the early 90s, don't judge).

"JESUS FUCK!!"—that was me.

The Shitbag owner had me pinned up against a stack of travertine while his hands groped my arse and tore at my clothes. My only path of escape came via the stacks of tiles. I launched myself back onto the top of thigh-high tiles, and the lecherous creep, thinking I was up for a bit of factory fucking, released his body weight from against me. Seizing the opportunity, I swung my legs over the stacks and landed on another side of the tiles. I pushed the top few layers of his $29 per meter lays toward him to further distract him and ran like I was on fire out of the humid factory. He was hollering after me that I wanted it; what else would I be doing visiting him at this time of night?

It was 6:12 pm on a Wednesday. Not exactly peak sexy time.

I didn't report it to my boss the next day. I didn't even consider calling the police. I just returned home and had a very, very long hot shower with lots and lots of exfoliation.

I've often thought about what I would have said if I had words and not been shocked into horrified silence.

"WHAT THE FUCK?!?"

"TAKE YOUR HANDS OFF ME, YOU GREAT VOMITOUS MASS" (I'm a Princess Bride Tragic)

"I'M GOING TO KICK YOUR BALLS THROUGH THE ROOF OF YOUR MOUTH!!!"

"COME AT ME MOTHERFUCKER!!"—Season with a breaking bottle, vase, trophy, fence paling....you get the idea, just WEAPON UP!

I like these responses. I enjoy these responses very much; thank you, and I think they can be the most excellent responses to workplace sexual harassment.

But sometimes, you can be rendered mute because of the cold disbelief that someone is touching your body without permission or has said something so wildly shocking.

And now, I have a stock standard reply that I have at the ready when I experience or see someone else suffering from fucked-up behaviour.

"That is not appropriate".

I know, I know it's a total comedown after the colourful and more vibrant put-downs listed above. But hear me out.

When caught off guard, your brain is flooded by a shedload of information. Your fight or flight response kicks in, your vital signs are amped up, your breathing labours, your brain is scanning for the quickest path out of dodge, and you're panicked. Those colourful replies I listed above? They came to me well after the actual event when I had time, space and a lecherous tile owner free space to formulate the perfect reply that would have stopped him in his tracks.

"That is not appropriate" is easy to remember when you are looking for ways to jettison yourself from the hell pit you've found yourself in. It applies to both in-person events as well as over the phone or social commenting. It can claim back your personal power or can be used to intercede on someone else's behalf when they are rendered mute by conduct that is out of order.

In short, it's the Allen key of responses to fucked up behaviour in the workplace. I prefer to use it like machine gun pellets: *"THAT. IS NOT. APPROPRIATE."* Add a steely gaze at the end. Don't be the first to break. Hold your nerve. Breathe. If the perp wants to engage you with further conversation, walk back what was said or done, justify, escalate, just take Lizzo's very sound advice and walk your fine arse right out that door.

"That is not appropriate" is not an invitation for further discourse. It's calling out unacceptable behaviour. Extract yourself as soon as it's safe, or you're able to do so and then gather support, tell someone about it what you've experienced, document the conduct or call a friend for support. To summarise—call the bad behaviour out and then seek support.

I have used *"That is not appropriate"* more times than I wish I had to.

- When hearing a bunch of white, middle-aged men talking trash to young female Chinese Uni students attempting to quickly board a train once the doors were opened.

- To a man who started to remove his trousers a few seats over from me, one late night train trip in an isolated carriage. (Trains…notice a pattern? Public transport for the masses, not a forum to behave like barnyard animals!)

- When being asked by a supplier if I enjoyed being on my knees as I was wedged under a desk at a site install using cable ties to tidy up the power and data leads.

- To the sketchy dude attempting to do a shakedown on my convenience store owner one rainy Sunday afternoon, telling them he would "protect" the store from other local crooks if he was paid in smokes and beer.

- BONUS! *"That is not appropriate"* is equal opportunity. To the woman who complained loudly to the train carriage (trains…I swear it brings out the worst in humanity) that people should speak English or "fuck off and go back to where they came from" to the group of young men speaking excitedly before their night out.

Try *"That is not appropriate"* on for size. Practise your delivery and your steady gaze. And then deploy at will. My hot tip is to try a train; bad behaviour is heavily over-represented there.

I IS FOR ILLNESS

There will probably be a time in your life when a loved one tells you that they have cancer or a chronic illness. For the sake of this chapter, I'll be referencing cancer, but what I suggest here also applies to any chronic illness or challenging health diagnosis.

When your loved one shares their health status with you, they will be scared, confused, overwhelmed, worried and... anxious about your reaction. So it's on you here to be the solid, stoic comfort that they are seeking. This does not mean you don't show emotion or remain mute, rigid in silence. Instead, I'd encourage you to follow the example of the lovely Lauren, who found out that one of her dear friends in her 20's got a cancer diagnosis that was not part of her five-year plan. Lauren works outside Washington and is a digital marketing maven. She's had a great past year, a loving partner, an awesome team, and has a juicy side gig writing fiction. But then this: an expected and shocking diagnosis, one of her friends in seemingly robust health has cancer...what possibly is there to say? What words can match the enormity of having cancer?

Lauren decided to say nothing. I don't mean she sat bolt upright in front of her friend as she processed this news and watched the clock creep by. She sat in the sadness and the confusion and the fear about what this cancer diagnosis meant and what the future held. It takes a lot of internal strength and self-control to sit with someone and not fill the silence with meaningless chatter or stories that are unrelated to the dilemma at hand. I've talked in other chapters about not retreating into silence when confronted with various scenarios, but there's a difference between active and passive silence. Passive silence is when you don't know what to say, so you say nothing, rather than even confessing you're lost for the right words. You retreat, perhaps avoid the person who confided in you, but all the while torturing yourself. You should be smart enough or wise enough to find the right words to say.

Active silence is something altogether different. It's doing the hard thing of sitting alongside someone who is going through something terrible. It might be sitting in a car with someone on a drive, your hand resting on their leg while you share the silence between you. It might be looking out at a stunning sunset together and letting the moment pass between you. You might even go for a walk in nature, silent marvelling at all the light filtering through the leaves of the bush. By being there, even in silence, you allow the opportunity for words to bubble up. The conversation that sparks might not be directly related to cancer but instead might be either mundane or profound. Or it could be about cancer…the point is that by opening up the space through silence and internal reflection, some words will surface in time, and you'll be there to catch them.

※ ※ ※

I've recommended active silence as one way to meet the cancer talk, but there are so many others like…

"I see...can you tell me what this cancer diagnosis means to you". A cancer diagnosis will usually involve a fuck load of technical words that sound confusing and steeped in medical jargon, so it's great to hear the person with cancer decipher them in their words.

"This is unexpected news...I'm going to pause for a second and just collect my thoughts." This approach is super helpful when you lose your shit or are scratching for words to say. The aim is not to mask your true feelings but to take a beat and then proceed forthwith, making your loved one the focus of your words and not to make it about you.

"I would guess that you have many people to share this news with...can I support you in this, and what might that look like for you?" Try to find a person in a first-world country that has not been touched by cancer. Actually, I'll save you the time so you can get back to listening to "Fear Inoculum" by Tool. There's not a damn person in a first-world country not touched by cancer. Either your close or extended family has been kicked in the nuts by it, or a close friend/member of your wider circle / a workmate has had the C-Bomb explode their life. So there are a lot of people to tell about cancer, and the level of sharing can vary from the total, ghastly truth to a more private sharing of "Tony is dealing with some complex health issues right now and will be working from home often". In helping share the news of the cancer diagnosis, it's good form to ask the person with cancer who they want to know about it and how much they are comfortable sharing. Don't be all about broadcasting this across the socials with prayer hands emojis and sending love and light; that shit is trite and not helpful. Instead, ask if you can help and then respect the wishes of the person with cancer.

"Would you like me to talk about something else besides

cancer?" I've heard from a number of people that when they have cancer, their body is open all hours for medical specialists and allied health professionals to work on. Every bodily function is scrutinised. You spend yonks hooked up to machines that are simultaneously trying to kill you and keep you alive. Blood is being drawn from your stressed veins, and everyone who knows you have cancer comes to you with a look of worry and soft, whispery voices. Perhaps your person with cancer needs a damn good laugh about you strutting through the office with your skirt tucked into your pantyhose. Maybe they need a night with sheet masks and Sauvignon Blanc. Maybe they'd like to go to the movies and lust over Idris Elba. Or maybe they want to talk about anything else but cancer... because cancer can go eat a big bag of dicks.

"If there's one thing that could help you now, what would that be?" It gets up the skirt that so many people's default response to bad news is to ask, "let me know if you need anything!" Insert prayer hand emoji. Da fuck? Why would you also assign more shit for someone to sort through when they are in the throes of extreme fuckery? Do not add to someone's to-do list through your laziness. I know the "one thing" seems to place the onus on the person with cancer to come up with something, but there are a few subtle differences here. Firstly, you're just asking for a single suggestion, and OF COURSE, you'd happily fill an entire grocery order for your person, but when someone is overwhelmed with cancer, and its treatment, one thing done for them could seem like a miracle. Need your washing pinned out on the line? Done. Want someone to take notes while you see a doctor so you can listen but have notes to refer to later? Handle that shit. Desiring a cheesecake for dinner? I'm already out the door. The added bonus to this query is giving agency to your person with cancer when so many things are happening TO them. This sweet offer is asking what can be

done FOR them; such a powerful shift back to focus on the person with cancer.

"Can I organise a schedule for transport to and from appointments/food deliveries/home care?" A person with cancer is up the jaxsie with appointments, and with more hospitals and cancer centres charging parking fees that would rival the annual GDP of a small nation, the idea of being picked up and dropped off could be very tantalising, especially if you're feeling nauseous and keen to see a friendly face. By offering to be the one to set up an excel spreadsheet and recruit supporters, you are doing your loved one with cancer a great service. With you handling the admin, they are free to focus on their treatment and recovery. Just be sure to get the Ok before you rock on with your spreadsheet, so you don't overstep boundaries.

"I'm here for you...now and throughout this phase of your life" So simple and so powerful, especially when with the added sweetener of being here for the long haul. When someone first announces they have cancer, there is a rush of activity and support, but after some time, the supporter's focus can revert back to the minutiae of daily life. For a person with cancer, it's conforming to hear that you'll be in the trenches with them for as long as it takes. Show up for the marathon, not the sprint.

※ ※ ※

Like a rabid Trump supporter in the queue for an all-you-can-eat deep-fried buffet, these rank words are best given a wide berth:

"Wow...I hope you don't die" When you're already nose to nose with the Great Beyond, you don't need some muppet to remind you that with all the treatment, cheesecakes and best care in the world, this might not be a "triumph over cancer story". You can think this, you can use this as a daily walking meditation, you can scream this into the pillow, but under no circumstances are you opening your pie hole and saying these words.

"Oh, cancer is the worst; let me tell you about my Uncle Morrie's cancer scare...." Every cancer story is unique, and what probe ended up in Uncle Morrie's butt may not be applicable to another's cancer journey. Now's not the time for charming stories about colostomy bags, hair that sheds like leaves falling in autumn, inexplicable body secretions and hateful Dr Lynn and her shitty bedside manner. Unless specifically asked, no stories, no grading of cancer stories about who has it worst. Shut the fuck up.

"Oh, you'll be FINE. I know how strong you are!" This is the fucked part about cancer. It doesn't matter how strong you are, how delightful you're to strangers and how much money you have donated to injured wildlife appeals. When cancer comes for you...it's a determined fucker. It's the ultimate equal opportunist. It will overlook race, age, disability, job profile, star sign and income bracket. When it comes for you, there's no gentle door knock; the door gets totally annihilated along with the rest of your life. Strength—perceived or otherwise—is a poor pre-determination for the cancer prognosis.

"You should join a cancer support group" At first glance, this seems sound advice, getting support from other people's cancer journey. Some folks will get so much inspiration and support from the various cancer groups; others will bristle at the over-saturation of pink that seems to be the mainstay of

breast cancer groups and charities. Or feel flattened if they don't share the view that cancer is a "battle to be defeated". The implication is that if you don't fight cancer valiantly enough, you're not the warrior you should have been. Let me tell you the story of my gorgeous friend Mindy. When Mindy first learned she had cancer decided to only tell her loving partner and parents. There was a total of 3 people who knew Mindy had cancer, and this was deliberate. Mindy knew that her rare cancer would consume so much of her energy, so she decided that she couldn't also manage the emotional responses of her friends and wider circle if they knew she had cancer. Mindy got centred so she was as calm and strong for her treatment as she could be and wasn't distracted by others' upsets, messages, well-intentioned advice and treating her as a cancer patient rather than her funny and capable friend Mindy. You might not agree with Mindy's approach, but a person with cancer must have agency, as so much of their lives is governed by treatment schedules and medical appointments.

"Have you tried kombucha to cure cancer?" My hunch is that you are not a medical professional, and you're not treating your person for cancer. If these assumptions are indeed correct, back the fuck up from recommending any alternate treatment, practitioner, retreat centre, ointment, essential oil, hemp wide-legged trousers or an all-raw diet. Many alternative therapies have their place in the treatment of cancer, but unless explicitly and lucidly requested by the person with cancer to provide reccie's put down your yoni beads and juicer and be a god damn real person. When you have cancer, advice is sprinkled like confetti over you, and while well-meaning, it rides a rough shot over the agency that the person with cancer has in their care and treatment. Be supportive and encouraging in the way they choose to manage their health. Respect the treatments they are taking from their health care team and resist any urge to weigh in with an electric juicer.

"Everything happens for a reason." The shit it does. There is no good reason for cancer, none. You can make meaning from a cancer diagnosis, but this is up to the person with cancer, not have fake-ass spiritual bullshit put upon you by a friend, family member or relative stranger who should know better.

"Your energy bought this on". OH, HELL NO!!! The law of attraction has a LOT to answer for, beginning with those shapeless tie-dyed sacks that people waft about in with a smug smile on their dial because they are "spiritual". No one wakes up, stares at their to-do list and thinks, "Awesome, looks like I have a space available for cancer!" While you can carry genes that are pre-disposed to cancer, and yes, certain behaviours like smoking can increase your chances of cancer even the shittiest energy field can not bring on cancer. Park this spiritual nonsense and check your desire to be energetically superior. And being a dick.

J IS FOR JEALOUSY

Jealousy might be a curse, but it's very, very instructive.

Us Scorpios are renowned for our diversions into jealousy. In our natural habitats, we're so placid and easy-going that I guess we have to have a tiny downside. Rather than being guilty and self-flagellating over feeling jealous of others or situations, I like to go a layer deeper than just letting the jealousy percolate on the surface. I've found that my jealous urges spike when I want what a person has, or they're experiencing. For example, when I was single for long stretches, I mooned over loved-up, nauseating couples on socials. No lie—they were nauseatingly smug and quite possibly even misrepresenting the level of connectedness they felt. But sitting under the jealous feeling was that I, too, wanted to feel loved and cherished. Being single, I couldn't look to a partner to provide this. I needed to do it for myself. I'd argue that you need to do this whether you're coupled up, single or in a status-fluid situation.

Some good words to ask yourself if you're feeling the jealousy rise to unhealthy levels:

"What is this jealousy trying to show me? Is it a feeling, experience, or wish I want for myself?" A good example is seeing your friends out on the tiles, snapping selfies and having a banger of a time on the socials. What's really going on—are you wanting to feel part of a group? Do you want to be out dancing and having fun? Do you want to be more visible on the socials and share more of yourself? Jealousy is such a cloak for so many other feelings and emotions. It's illuminating to dive deep and uncover what's yearning for.

"Can I remove myself from this situation and choose another feeling?" Being blinded by jealousy is a really uncomfortable feeling. It screws with our perceptions. Suddenly, your partner innocently chatting with the barista over their morning coffee being brewed becomes a full-blown sexual dalliance complete with arseless chaps and rivers of lube. If you feel the jealousy ratcheting up, can you divert your attention from the moment? Can you choose another feeling like grace, forgiveness for others—or yourself—or even settle on neutral observation? Taking a beat to choose another feeling will help diffuse the situation and stop you from going nuclear on the barista for propositioning your partner over a hot chai all before 7:30 am.

"So what?" Your brain can throw up some messed up shit. You don't have to indulge it or jolly it along. Sometimes you can interrupt the slide into jealousy and darker emotions by simply asking it...so what? So what if I think my partner is getting hot sex from the barista? So what if my friends went out last Saturday night without me and had a riot of a time? So what? So what? It's a good question to ask as your brain is usually pretty good at providing status reports, fanciful

scenarios, and negative commentary on your day...but less skilled at answering disarming questions like "so what?

✦ ✦ ✦

But, what I hear you ask is, do you say if you suspect jealousy has afflicted a counterpart, a lover or an associate? You're feeling the pointed barbs from your interactions with them, and hell, they may have even typed "HAAAAAAAATE U BALL BAG" under your latest update on the socials. How do you counteract the jealous type?

"You seem a little tense / terse with me—what's going on?" Jealousy can appear as snide comments, accusatory tones, pointed accusations or even strained silence. Acknowledge the feeling that hangs in the air and ask them straight up— what's the story, morning glory?

"You've mentioned that you're the jealous type in the past. Is that what's going on for you here?" Most self-aware types like my fella G know they are predisposed to jealousy, so if this is your person, ask them if that's what they're experiencing now. I've never had to ask this of G; bless him. Being in and out of La Vida Pandemic Lockdown for two years, the only other regular presence in my life apart from him was Ben and Jerry's ice cream, and G is cool with me bringing this other love of mine into the relationship as long as I don't hog the spoon.

"I don't like how you're treating me. It's not ok. Please stop." This is a good one where you really don't have the bandwidth to deal with someone else's drama. You don't want or need

the backstory of their jealousy. You just want them to knock it off. Your time is precious, and you get to decide who you spend time on—and those you don't. You're not the Manly Ferry; you're not taking passengers.

J IS ALSO FOR JOBS

Perhaps you've heard of the great resignation, a phenomenon where employed people emerged from their Covid caves and said, "This job thing? It sucks, and I'm not going to spend a moment more with a passive-aggressive boss that thinks it's amusing to undermine my contribution in every meeting". The phenomena have led to large swathes of the workforce changing roles and industries or winding back their hours to enjoy life more or start their own side gigs. With the great resignation underway, those people leaving their jobs mostly look for another job, so it begs the question: how do you find a job that's a good fit for you, will develop your skills, allow you to make a meaningful contribution and won't shit you to tears. Well, there's the job advertisement route, or grabbing opportunity by the short and curlies and asking for the job you want.

This might look like approaching someone you know working for a company you feel aligned with and asking if there are roles on offer you could be recommended for. Or perhaps it's sending in your snazzy resume, perfectly tailored to showcase the value you'd add to your dream company's culture and bottom line.

If you're running a business and want to work with a client, send them a "Shock and Awe" pack that will have them reaching for the phone before they finish reading your cover letter to set up a meeting. The "Shock and Awe" pack is an idea, by John Blake, from Sales Breakthrough Solutions to cut through the cold-call crap companies are swamped with. I was looking to ditch my consulting gig in the trade-show industry and take on entire sales office fit-out projects. John suggested packaging up a professionally printed portfolio of my work and writing a letter to the client explaining how I could help them with their particular sales office fit-out challenge. I added a box of delicious handmade chocolate truffles to the pack as an added sweet surprise. Those "Shock and Awe packs, personally couriered and addressed to the decision-maker in the company I wanted to work for, have earned me at least $6 million from that client so far, a $120 investment. The ROI from the "Shock and Awe" pack has been astonishing and continues to secure my business converted clients and projects.

I know it can be really confronting putting yourself out there and risking rejection if the play to secure your next gig, secure a coveted client or have you blissed out with a new role falls flat. But what if it gets you the role or the client you desire? Maybe you don't get the job straight away, but your direct approach was memorable enough for the firm to keep your details on file and call you up next time a position comes up that's a perfect fit. Maybe you don't get the dream client with your "Shock and Awe" pack because the incumbent is doing a great job, but you get a valuable connection, so when the contact goes to their next role, you're asked to come in and pitch for their work.

Pull your shoulders back, channel your best version of J-Lo, making power moves and try these on for size when doing a cold call. Oh, and if you're on the phone making this approach, smile as you talk, it makes such a difference to how you one across to the other person. You can hear the warmth and friendliness through the phone line.

"Hi [their name—do your research about who's the best person to speak to within the company you're approaching]. I'm [your name—always personalise your calls/emails, so you're not just another caller interrupting their day], and I'm calling to introduce myself. I've been following your company for some time, and I really like how you value your staff / are doing a lot of meaningful work in aged care / using cutting-edge technology to improve recycling [include what you're seeing the company do well and applaud them for it, compliments never get old]. I'd really love the opportunity to work in your company, and I'm reaching out to see if there are any current opportunities or if something might be coming up in the future?" You don't have to produce an essay in the initial contact; you aim for friendly and memorable—and the direct approach will do that every time over an email that gets lost in the day-to-day detritus.

The true gold in any cold approach to a job or an opportunity is in the follow-up. Even if it's a no—don't give up, especially if you just know in your heart this company is part of your future. Diarise a follow-up in a few weeks after you have sent through your resume or "Shock and Awe" pack and see if there are any questions about what you sent through or if things have changed since you last spoke. Going after your dream—be it in life, career or business takes tenacity. Keep going after those dreams and stoke those ambitions. As far as we know, we only get one chance at life, so make it so amazing it stuns even you.

K IS FOR KINDNESS

If I see another social email post expounding "be kind", I'm likely to cut a bitch.

This social media post usually follows a monumental clusterfuck by the poster who has had their ableist/sexist/racist/homophobic/right-wing nutcracker views challenged. And let me be clear about this—there is abso-fucking-lutely an ocean-size gap between bullying and constructive criticism of viewpoints and behaviours. If you can't spot the difference between "You're a stupid bitch" and "Your views on white privilege are not well-formed, and you need to do further study on why you don't see yourself as benefitting from the power structures of whiteness", then take several seats and pull out some good reads to educate yourself.

You can have a debate without name-calling. You can be criticised without it being a personal attack. You can hold a contradictory point of view without the self-conscious justification of your standpoint and the trashing of others. And you can be kind without lapsing into continually defending yourself. You can be kind and still argue with a loved one. You can be kind because it's almost always the perfect fallback position. Please remember that kindness is not only for others. It's meant for you as well.

I was in New Orleans at the Louis Armstrong International Airport, which curiously seemed to have no flights to international locations unless you count Newark as an overseas destination. It was early morning, still dark, and I arrived the obligatory 3 hours before my flight so I could prepare to do the progressive striptease through security to prove I had not concealed a semi-automatic or harpoon on my person. Sitting outside a newsagency, tapping away on my laptop and eating a delicious breakfast of Reece's Pieces, I became aware that a young man on a seat against mine was silently sobbing.

I closed my laptop and took a pause...should I....? "I'm sorry to interrupt", I began softly. "But are you ok?" This made him cry harder, and he turned to me, face red through his tears, and he shook his head. "Would you like to talk about it?" I inquired. His head shook harder, and he choked out, "I... can't!" I nodded my head, my face full of concern. "I understand; it's ok", I reassured him. "But if it's ok with you, I'm just going to sit here with you in case you need to talk." He nodded through the sobs. "Are you ok if I rest my hand on your shoulder?" I asked. He nodded again, quicker. And so we sat silently like that for probably 30 minutes, my hand on his shoulder, sometimes squeezing it, sometimes patting it gently[8].

His state of distress gradually receded over time, and the sobs lessened. After some time, I ventured, "Do you have someone that you trust that you can be with?" He nodded, and he told me he was going to visit his dad. We sat for a little longer, and his flight was called. For the first time, he looked directly at me. "Thank you", he said quietly. "I'm glad I was here," I told him honestly. "I'll be keeping you in my thoughts and hoping for better days ahead for you". He gripped my hand, and the space that exists between strangers evaporated. A person in need reached out to another in distress, and they were met with kindness and stillness. I didn't need to know that day what had upset the young man so badly, but what I did understand was that in that moment, he needed another, and I was that person. I think of him often, and I've held true to that promise that I hope he enjoyed better times from the highly emotional state he was in that day.

You can be kind to strangers, too; not everyone wants to scam or catfish or make a skin suit from you, despite what the multitudes of streaming documentaries display on television.

※ ※ ※

Try these ideas:

Smile to retail staff, your barista, the serving staff, the concierge and most especially dogs. Hell, just smile at everyone. Catch the eye of someone you pass by and grin. Masks are a part of modern life, so turn up the smile wattage so your eyes crinkle and your face above any mask you might be wearing, light up. So many of us are held hostage by our phones, heads permanently bowed as we move through the day, so when someone smiles at us, it's noticed, especially to the strangers who make our day go smoother: smile and mean it.

"Can I help you with that?" Seeing someone struggle with their shopping, luggage, opening a door or finishing off a piece of chocolate cake? Ask first before assisting. Don't sweep in and start taking over. It can be terribly disempowering for someone, especially if they are elderly or disabled, to have people wanting to help (despite the best of intentions) without asking for permission first. And if they say

no, respect that and wish them well. Please don't be like the man who insisted that I needed his help moving a suitcase and we were locked in a push-me-pull-you situation over a wheelie bag, while I insisted, "I GOT THIS, SIR! SIR, RELEASE MY BAG!"

"I'm Fiona. What's your name?" This is an unexpected one but one that I've used a number of times to get myself out of a stack of sticky situations. Using my name and asking for someone else's, brings the other person back into the moment and emphasises our humanity. I've used this in countries—with the appropriate translation—where English is not the dominant language. I've used this to diffuse tense situations in bars and on public transport when things have gotten heated, and I've used it when attending to someone who requires first aid. You got a name—you got leverage. And by having their name, you can sprinkle this in conversation to build that connection with another.

L IS FOR THE LOSS OF A LOVED ONE

If you ever want to shut down a conversation or render someone mute, tell them you've just experienced the death of a loved one.

Pin. Drop.

On any given day in Australia, there's a death every 3 mins and 12 seconds. That's a lot of bereaved people stumbling around, clutching tissues and having their hearts put through the shredder. With death being the inevitable outcome of life, it's a wonder that western cultures—largely—are not better at talking, thinking and preparing for it. I totally understand the bypass we want to do when it comes to thinking about the deaths of ourselves or our loved ones; it's an uncomfortable topic. Death is the inevitable end game of life, so best we get some strategies in place for coping with it.

No one wants the spectre of "Oh, this will all be over soon or when I least expect it" when celebrating events, sharing good times or enjoying a meal with like-minded folk. However, I do think the observation of death can help you decide what really is important in life. It can hone your desire to go after your most precious dreams, spend time with the people that matter and make you drop your shit as nothing else can.

I'm lucky that as I write this, both my elderly parents are alive and in rather rude health thanks to the healthy consumption of Neenish Tarts over the years. I'm making even more of an effort to spend time with them, free from Covid lockdowns, as I see my mum's mobility recede, and I know the bulk of our time together has passed, and I'm in the residuals now. I've thought about the deaths of my parents. I've stepped through the likely feelings and the process that happens once they've passed. I've stage-rehearsed how I will tell my friends and other family members how they died. I've practised the words I will say to my nieces to comfort them and the recollection of memories I'll hold to help me navigate the times after their deaths. And yet...I'm nowhere near ready to have them die.

I think part of the reason we're so shit at death is when someone dies; we've been reminded of our own infallibility as well as the mortality of others that we love so dearly. Suddenly, the stench of death is everywhere, and while the pain of losing this person is so real and raw, what are you to do when death comes calling for another that you hold dear? What if it's not old age that death is attributed to and largely accepted as the way things go? Instead, its death through the jolting shock of an accident, suicide, miscarriage, homicide or a sudden illness. Even if death was somewhat expected, it still arrives like a cannonball through your life, pulverising the slim grasp you believe you had on reality.

In 2002 I lost my person, J, to suicide. Perhaps this might only be understood by those mourning a loved one through suicide, but it was both the shock of my life and entirely a likely outcome of J's tumultuous life story. 2002 was before the internet was really in full flight, so information and support for someone bereaved through suicide were thin on the ground. Suicide support services were harder to access and difficult to locate. We were definitely in the time pre "Are You Ok Day?" and suicide was still a taboo topic.

I can remember seeing a client's visible recoil like I was contagious when I explained I'd had time off from work due to the loss of J through suicide. I recall a dear friend saying, "aren't you over this yet" when at a restaurant for dinner, uncontrolled tears slipped down my cheeks. My dad, who was struggling with the loss of J too, offered, "Well, at least you can get on with your life now". Strangers and loved ones will all struggle with the news of you suffering the loss of a loved one. Try not to let it sting too much. We're all trying and most likely failing to provide real comfort because there's no comfort that will ever soothe the shock of losing someone to suicide.

Here are some things you can say that will be helpful and meaningful to the bereaved:

"I'm so sorry to hear this news. How are you? What comfort, like food, calling others to let them know, or even me coming to sit with you, would be most helpful?" The phrase "let me know if there's anything I can do" makes me want to flip occasional tables. The last thing anyone wants to do when they've suffered the loss of someone is to add more load to the mental stress they're carrying. I get why people say to contact them if they can be of help, but best you provide some options to them of things you'd be happy to help provide. Please don't offer to cook meals when your culinary skills extend as far as picking up the cheapest pizza

in your neighbourhood. Likewise, if kids aren't your jam, don't offer to supervise them while funeral preparations are being made. Please offer in ways that you'd be satisfied to provide. And remember to ask how the bereaved person is. We're naturally curious creatures, so we often spend a lot of time wanting to understand the cause, timing and events surrounding death. We forget the person that's here and struggle to understand how to get through the next hour without their loved one.

"Can I be with you? We don't even have to talk, but I'd like to be there in case you do and for some company". One of the most helpful things that a friend of mine, Claire, did for me when J died was for her to come to my place and be with me after I heard the news that J had taken his own life. I was mute from the shock; tears would not stop falling as I tried to make sense that I now lived while my beloved was cold and dead. Claire didn't try and explain it away or trot out the well-meaning but hollow "it all happens for a reason". She held my hand, passed fresh tissues, got me water and was strong enough to bear my grief. I'll be forever grateful for that.

"Keep them in your heart, always" This is attributed to my mum. She's legendary for having a drawer full of cards for every occasion that can be popped in the mail to mark an occasion or a passing. This beautiful statement is simple and heartfelt. Feel free to use it both for others and for yourself. It's the perfect phrase for both in-person and written words of comfort.

Please give these words a short shift:

"They're in a better place". What, Hawaii? The sentiment is coming from a good place, but for any tone that's stinging from the loss of a loved one, that best place is always alive and right by their side.

"They are now free of pain". Good for them. That pain has now been dispersed to the people that loved and cared for them, and it's theirs to carry. Losing a loved one to suicide is a special sort of agonising grief. Guilt overlays so many other emotions. What did I miss? What more could I have done? If only I had one more day with them. Being reminded that your loved one has moved beyond this world of pain is no help. Because you're all too aware of the accused and the relentless pain, you're in because they are no longer here.

"Suicide is such a selfish act". I've thought a lot about J and his suicide over the years. And I've never felt compelled to describe it as selfish. Other people that I've spoken with who faced the loss of someone to suicide have agreed. Our loved ones chose suicide as a way of ending the pain and suffering they were experiencing. They believed they were doing the people that loved them a favour by exiting this life as they felt like a burden on others. I would never describe J as a weight that dragged me lower. We all land in different places with losing a loved one to suicide, but I believe J saw suicide as a selfless act, even though I disagree vehemently with this view. He decided to "free" his loved ones from being tormented by seeing him so disconnected from the joy of living. It pains people who have lost someone through suicide to hear them described as selfish. To be in such torment and decide the only option is to end your life demands compassion and not judgement.

M IS FOR MEDICAL STUFF

A few years ago, I had a cyst on my labia. And I did what any person vigilant about their health and well-being does. I ignored it and gloried on with my life.

This was a deeply flawed plan as I was tits deep in rowing season. Rowing is renowned for being an all-over-body sport, and after rowing for several weeks with that bastard cyst on my labia, I wholeheartedly concur. Sitting on that rowing seat and knocking out around 9 km during a pre-dawn session really cooked that cyst good. It got to the point where I was sitting side-saddle while doing computer work and during in-person meetings to avoid the pain of putting any pressure on that cyst. Shit had got real, and I needed to take action.

I made an appointment with a local medical centre. I couldn't get to see my regular female doctor as she was on leave, but at this point, I didn't care too much who I saw; I needed relief and FUCKING NOW.

I gingerly climbed onto the examination bed, so this new female doctor could take a look at the cyst. Being naked from the waist down in the presence of a stranger will make the most resilient person feel wretched. To cover for my nervousness, I was rabbiting on about the cyst when I noticed it, the increase in pain and how I hoped it would be an easy fix. Like maybe some ointment? Or even a tablet? I'm also good with a healing sound bath, so sign me up for that.

Reader. None of those options was on offer. The doctor barely acknowledged me or asked any questions. She pulled at me roughly while I tried to focus on the fingers of light coming through the Venetian blinds that covered the window above the bed where I lay.

Suddenly, I let out a blood-curdling cry of pain as the doctor squeezed the cyst without warning. I involuntarily reached up and yanked down the entire Venetian blind as I was wracked with waves of pain and nausea. The moment passed, the pain was slowly subsiding, and I sat half upright, panting with the blind still in my hands. The doctor said nothing. She stared at me in shock, blinking rapidly.

"Sorry about your blind," I said as I handed her the destroyed blind. I finished dressing and half-staggered out of her consultation room. I realised later they had forgotten to charge me for the appointment. But then, I figured it was a fair outcome given the pain I experienced due to the non-consent for cyst squeeze. And the total annihilation of her Venetian blind.

My experience with the cyst was one of the few less-than-optimal interactions I'd had with the health service. The majority of my experiences have been positive and respectful. We've come a long way from doctors being seen as gods, and now the overwhelming majority of health professionals see the patient and the professionals as working as a team together to work towards better health outcomes.

My friend Lizzie is one of those medical types with very big brains who is now involved with mentoring and teaching the next generation of medical professionals to communicate with a real live person and not treat them as a cadaver.

I love what Lizzie shared with me recently about how she encourages her charges to clarify what they have just explained to their patient.

"I want to be sure that I've explained myself clearly and I haven't missed anything or said something you might not have understood. Can you repeat back to me what you've heard me say?"

Big brain...I tell you. This is genius. Let's break it down.

"I want to be sure that I've explained myself clearly": The health professional assumes the responsibility for making the information succinct and able to be understood. They recognise that the burden of transferring information to the patient is on them; it's not on the patient to have a working knowledge of medical terms or diagnoses. It's also placing the health professional and the patient on the same level. It's not the health professional in the authority position, which can be intimidating for a lot of people, including those that have been traditionally marginalised by western medicine. This approach opens the door to the non-judgmental sharing of information that can be processed and not send the patient into a tailspin.

"Can you repeat back to me what you heard me say"? Again, this is gold. It gives the patient a chance to put into their own words what they have heard. The health professional then can determine if there are any gaps in their interpretation or if areas need to be expanded upon or clarified.

✸ ✸ ✸

If you're in the hot seat and about to have a conversation with a medical professional about your care and well-being, here are some other good words you can say:

"I'm going to take notes as you speak". My first go-to is to take a trusted friend or family member along for the big health conversations. My sister and I do this for our ageing parents. One or sometimes both of us will attend an appointment with them, and we'll be the scribes while our parents are free to ask questions and digest the responses. The officious note-taking also allows everyone to keep their own notes on their health history and refer to them later when they think, "Ok, did the doctor say that I had a Bartholin cyst on my lady parts or was it a Gartner type cyst?" Do I need to panic shop and buy all the expensive La Mer face creams or do I need to chill and know in time the cyst will rectify itself?" If you don't have a person to attend an appointment with you or a serious talk is sprung on you, it's cool! Take some notes that you can workshop with a loved one after the appointment.

"If I need further information, where or who do I go to for that". It's impossible to flush out all queries in the typical allotted 20 min medical appointment. So get the good oil on where you can get follow-up information—the health professional might recommend themselves, an associate or another allied health practitioner. And don't discount support groups for various health issues. Having the support and guidance of someone whose been through the same diagnosis that you have is enormously comforting.

"What's the plan from here?" Action trumps everything. It applies doubly to managing health issues. If you're managing a life-altering diagnosis, you want to know what the next move is. Even small health complaints will trigger some sort of treatment and care. It might be as straightforward as a course of antibiotics or performing a series of exercises at home to recover from injury. Regardless, you'll need to participate in your own care and well-being. So sort that shit out and start working on a plan with your healthcare team. Even the direst of diagnoses can be made bearable knowing that there's a plan to look after both your diagnosis and you as a beautiful human.

M IS ALSO FOR MISCELLANEOUS

The quick-fire round!

* A hostile nation ruled, but a drunk-with-power, unhinged overload whose hobbies include bare-chested wrestling of bears (I'm strongly and forever Team Bear), invades your sovereign, peaceful nation that was minding its own damn business. What can you possibly say? *"Go fuck yourself!"* Mad respect to the most resilient, brave and wiliest people on the planet, the Ukrainians.

* If someone complains about the state of the nation, the politicians, policies relating to the environment, aged care, gun control and the treatment of refugees (for starters), please, do ask, *"Do you vote?"* Because if you don't, you forfeit the right to complain. You might think that one person can affect much change but as some champ pointed out at the height of the Covid pandemic, tell that to someone who once ate a half-cooked bat. Voting is both a right and a privilege, so make sure you're adding your voice to shaping how your nation is governed.

* Instead of being out and about in the world, refrain from immersing yourself in your smartphone as a means of

distraction. Try the radical idea of engaging with another human. Perhaps you think of them as very cute and possibly good company. Or maybe you want to reach across the divide and have a conversation with a real, live human. But how do you start a conversation and not seem creepy or do that thing where a stranger seems overly friendly but soon you discover they are soliciting for a monthly sign-up for Greenpeace? My go-to: *"Hey, what was the last thing that made you laugh out loud?"*. Another one I like, *"What are you looking forward to?"* And because I worship at the Church of Rock n' Roll: *"Got any recommendations for good music or live gigs?"* All of us can do with my laughter, hope and good tunes in our lives and maybe the inspiration from another will spark something in you.

✺ To those pesky charity collectors who always call when you're applying winged eyeliner: *"No thank you, please remove me from this call list"*, and hang up. I know some people use the opportunity to berate the caller and rip into them for wasting donation dollars. But I take no joy from making someone feel bad about calling on behalf of a charity soliciting donations to help pay the fucking energy bill of someone who's not doing so flash. Keep yourself nice and remember, we've all done jobs that someone else considers questionable or morally repugnant.

✺ *"Look, it's not for me, but I get that other person really digs it."* Useful for when someone is trying VERY hard to talk you into seeing a band you detest, try food that makes you nauseous, perform a sex act that you're not comfortable with or see art that makes you want to stab your eyes with a sharp pencil. It's good—actually, it's GREAT that we don't all like the same things. It creates a rich tapestry of diverse interests and preferences that make humans so interesting. Sometimes you encounter another who so very dearly wants to convince you of the correctness of their viewpoint. A simple "no thanks" will not satiate them. Telling them upfront that you're not picking up what they're putting down and following that with an acknowledgment that others might be hankering for it will send the most rabid fan happily on their way.

"I'm so sorry you're upset with our product/service. I'm here to resolve the situation/issue. Can you please take me through what happened? Is it ok if I ask questions if I need more information?" No matter what business you're in or if you own your own gig, work in the public service or are an employee, someone sometime will complain. It's totally normal to want to avoid this conversation or cringe internally, but this situation is best handled pronto, not left to simmer. I find the apology upfront helps soothe dissatisfaction. Then, let them know you're the person that can help them. Next, ask for a recap, so you hear in their words what they're upset about. Finally, ask for permission to ask clarifying questions throughout rather than annoy them with unexpected interjections. At the end of the conversation, please let the person with the complaint know what the next steps are. Are you getting back to them in 48 hours? Are you shipping them another product? Even if you don't have an immediate resolution for them, say that and let them know when you will be in touch with an update. People can handle disappointment, lousy service or products that don't work as intended. What is guaranteed to fire them up and hit the socials with 1-star reviews and drag your company across the interwebs is when you don't address issues proactively or don't follow up.

✺ Ah, but what happens when you need to make a complaint? How do you manage your frustration levels, so they don't reach Mt Vesuvius levels of anger and agitation? Well, you use your words. *"Hi, I'm {Insert your name} and I'd like to speak to someone who can help me with a complaint I have about your product/service/person"*. And then stick to the facts when talking to the person assisting you. No name-calling, no threats of sticking your lawyer brother-in-law Morrie onto them, no promises to slander their name on the socials. Stay calm and have an idea and reasonable outcome in mind (no first-class tickets to Jamaica requests to make up for lack of inflight entertainment on your last flight. Honey, please, you'll be lucky if they sling you a complimentary bag of nuts from the food trolley to make up for not being able to stream Succession) that you'd accept as restitution. I find it's helpful to think of complaints as not whingeing but rather giving feedback to companies and people to be able to make good and do better. Certainly, this is the way I've framed it when I've (rightly) had complaints that bought my attention in the way my company was servicing our clients. It gave my staff and me the chance to review our internal processes and provide an even greater level of service. If you're committed to doing great work, you're going to need to level up and pay attention to complaints and negative feedback. Having clients and customers provide this feedback on where you might be missing the mark is the best sort of free-market analysis available.

N IS FOR NO WORDS

As much as I advocate for not shying away from having hard or tricky conversations, there are times when saying nothing is just as powerful.

Times like:

- When you need a moment—or even a period of time—to collect your thoughts, so you're able to provide a response that is meaningful and true to you.

- When you're already emotionally raw, and you know you'll be speaking out of frustration and could intensify an already brittle situation.

- When you know nothing is gained by rehashing the issue. You've stated your viewpoint, the other party has defined theirs, and presently, there's no common ground.

- When you feel a conversation is better had in-person / via the phone or text rather than in the current setting you're in. You might feel more comfortable saying what you need to in person, or you might prefer to write down your thoughts so they don't come out muddled.

- When you feel you're in an unsafe situation. It's paramount you look after yourself first and foremost.

- The situation is overwhelmingly heartbreaking, and words seem to have no meaning.

- You feel that the emotional burden is on you to always be the one to broker peace, mend fences and be the dependable one. If that weighs on you, perhaps opt out of the initiator of conversations and see if the other parties step up to do the heavy lifting.

- So now what? No words might come up for you, or you feel that it's not the time to talk. Here are some things that you could do instead:

- Sit with another person in silence. Just bearing witness and ensuring that your person is feeling less alone is a powerful gesture to another or a gift to yourself.

- Send flowers, a card or a text that has a simple message of "thinking of you and hoping that you're feeling more like yourself soon".

- Put an auto-responder on your email or change your message on your phone, letting people know you're ok, you're taking some time for yourself, and you'll be in touch when you feel able.

- You owe no one anything so if you want to descend into your pillow fort with potato chips and wine as a radical act of self-care, do so. But it might help to let a few trusted friends or family members know of this plan, so you don't have the cops come and do a welfare check on you.

- Make a meal, pick their kids up, walk the dog or offer to cover their work while your loved one is feeling poorly. Not everyone feels comfortable using words in times of strife, but simple acts of caring can provide comfort of their own.

- I have periods of anxiety where even trying to explain to another sends me into spirals of overwhelm, so I've come up with a plan on how to convey this feeling to my man-friend G without having him overly concerned for me. I tell him, "I have no words right now but trust that as soon as I do, I'll come to you". And once the anxiety freight train has hurtled by, I do come to G and share with him why I've been living on my last nerve. This pause helps me observe my feelings of anxiety rather than being tits deep in them. As such, it's easier to find the words to explain the experience rather than do the silent scream that the artist Munch made so infamous.

- Sit in the sun, pat an animal, lie on the grass, and walk on the beach. Being in nature or being around animals are great mood shifters for the majority of people. No words are required.

O IS FOR

OWNERSHIP OR OWNER-SHIT (OWN YOUR OWN SHIT AND LEAVE OTHERS TO DO SIMILARLY)

My friend Andrea is one of the smartest people I know. Firstly, she's a doctor and secondly, she once hiked in the Canadian wilderness for 2 months because she likes wonderfully weird shit. Oh, and she also wrestled a bear*.

* Probably. Here's where I add some flavour to the stories, author's prerogative and all that.

Because Andrea's career has been mainly in the scientific and medical fields, she is ridiculously talented in the realm of succinct and considered communication. No way can you drone on with meandering instructions and vague instructions when people's health and well being is on the line. You want clean and concise communication from your medical and scientific peeps.

"As your ethical adviser, I'm telling you clearly that if you proceed with that protocol you'll be in breach of the faculty guidelines and therefore open to disciplinary action". This gets you to stand up straight and put down that rabbit you were about to inject blue dye into.

"Heyyyyyyyyy…heard about some whacked out trial you were thinking of doing and I'm not wanting to crush your vibe and come down all heavy like but could you um, see your way to... well, you know, do it but different-like. Yeah?" This type of muddled messaging gets you a confused scientist AND a confused rabbit.

I once took two weeks to unravel a story about why my boyfriend and I had broken up. This swirling narrative was conveyed to Andrea over numerous fraught phone calls, long walks in the late afternoon haze and over-thick slabs of chocolate cake in Melbourne cafes. The breakup story lasted longer than the god damn relationship! Still, Andrea was attentive and thoughtful in her appraisal of the situation.

"He sounds like an idiot." Yeah, her bang on assessment doesn't even deserve an exclamation mark.

Andrea has recently given me a great communication checkpoint that is super easy to put into practice. Not only does it help you sharpen your communication, but it also has the added bonus of establishing boundaries and defining what is yours to own in any situation.

In helping me understand this concept, Andrea told me the story of her new boss joining the organization where she worked. The role had been unfilled for some time so when the appointment was made, Andrea and her team were excited to finally have someone in the leadership role and began preparing briefing documents and reports ready for the head of the organization to review when they started. By being on the front foot, they reasoned that this would help their leader make decisions quickly and then they could all get busy rolling our programs and completing projects that had stalled while they had been without leadership for several months.

The first day for the new leader comes and despite the team looking hopefully at anyone who walks in into their office... the new leader does not arrive. Later that day an email arrives to advise that he's sick and is postponing his first day for a week to get well. The team are disappointed but is understanding. During the week he's off ill, they fine-tune their project briefs and add even more content to their information-dense reports.

The following week...success! The leader arrives and introduces himself to the team. Clearly, he's been sick but hey, he's here, he's pleased to meet the team and is keen to know more. Andrea, looking to book time with him to brief him on her work and secure needed signs off for her projects and her KPIs, has several thoughts cascaded forth.

He's been sick.

Everyone wants time with him.

He's new and this is his first day.

He's barely found his desk...

And she sits back down in her office and decides to wait for him to approach her. Most of us would do the same. As humans, we're very attuned to people's suffering and difficult situations. That doesn't mean we're necessarily good at dealing with them but our emotional antenna certainly lets us know what's up. But Andrea is not most people. She's got a master craftsperson's certificate in boundary building. She catches herself in the story making of someone's situation and while all these things might be true of her boss...

He's been sick.

Everyone wants time with him.

He's new and this is his first day.

He's barely found his desk...

These observations contributed to Andrea's story of "my boss does not have time to deal with my pressing issues".

But he hasn't even had a chance to articulate to Andrea any challenges he's facing because they haven't even had a conversation yet!

Andrea reminds herself that her boss's ill health is not her job. Her job is to deliver on the ethics of the research facility. And that requires input from her boss. She crafts a short, pointed email to her boss about making a time to meet to discuss her projects and leaves the timing of the meeting for him to schedule. Within the hour, the boss sends a meeting request to Andrea and they're good to chat.

How often do we do this? We weave elaborate stories about situations and people based on scant evidence while avoiding the thing that would actually move us and our work forward. As difficult as managing ill health is, Andrea, recognised that her boss is a fully functioning adult able to make informed decisions and take ownership of his actions and therefore has agency over whether his recovery allows him to take a meeting.

Andrea owns the responsibility to deliver on ethical matters relating to the research facility.

Her boss has the ownership to review Andrea's projects, and provide feedback, direction and resources.

See how clear things become and we gain forward momentum when we stick to what we own and ditch the stories?

"For my project on the testing of new hearing devices in infants, I need you to sign off on this protocol so we can begin the initial on-boarding process" is sure as shit a lot more proactive and operating from a place of strength than "Oh, I won't bother him with my needs, I'll just wait for him to contact me".

Know what is yours to take ownership of and what is owner-shit. Execute from that solid base foundation.

✺ ✺ ✺

Other helpful thought interrupters when you start to spiral and take owner-shit of things that are not yours to carry:

- ✺ I need to stay in my lane.
- ✺ I just need to do the next right thing to move ahead.
- ✺ This is not my circus, these are not my monkeys.
- ✺ Nope, not today Satan.
- ✺ I need to slow my roll…what's really going on here?
- ✺ Am I operating from fact or my own fiction?
- ✺ Progress, not perfection

These types of owner-shit thought loops are best side-stepped:

- Why doesn't anyone seem to understand what I need?

- I'm stupid, I should be able to work this out.

- Why does everyone seem to have an easier time of it than I do?

- I must have offended or upset them, that's why they're avoiding talking to me.

- I'm just going to assume…

- I'm going to go read the comments of the inflammatory social media post so I feel good about my fellow humans. Yah, humans are the best!

- I'll just sit here and wait for something to happen.

P IS FOR PREGNANT PAUSES

I've never been pregnant. Therefore I'm an excellent and trustworthy authority on what to say and what to avoid when it comes to pregnancy.

Firstly—and this is of vital importance—you must never comment on a woman's mid-sections and say enthusiastically, "Hey, when is the baby due?!?" Women's bodies expand and contract for seemingly the most benign reasons. Shit, I had an epic burrito during the past week, and I have passed for carrying a life preserver ring under my waistband. So under no circumstance, even if you were in the room during conception, are you to link a woman's shape with the conclusion that they are pregnant. Sure, once they mention it, it's game on molls, but until then, mind your damn business and turn your attention to building a social media platform that does not foster untruths and unchecked conspiracy "theories".

So many well-meaning people have been caught in the bear trap of commenting on a women's pregnancy only to find out...they are not pregnant. Or maybe they are pregnant, but due to previous experiences of not being able to carry a baby to term, they're being circumspect in announcing it. Or perhaps they are not able to keep the baby. So many complex reasons for a woman not declaring her pregnancy, and every one of them is valid.

Now that we've established it's only possible to mention pregnancy when the other party does first, what other ways can we avoid making a goose of ourselves?

- Please don't touch the pregnant belly unless otherwise invited to do so. I know we feel that if we rub or touch the pregnant belly, next week, lotto numbers will be revealed to us. However, unsolicited touch has been—rightfully—gone the way of a penny-farthing bicycle. As in, been consigned to the WTF footnote in history. Pregnant bellies are not public property. Keep your greasy mitts to yourself.

- Don't launch into a story about how your own pregnancy—or pregnancy you know of—ended in complications, prolapse, strange spider veins on your thighs or that the baby comes out looking more like a small hairy Wooly mammoth. I'm not saying you can't share these stories, but like a courteous driver, please yield to another party. If they mentioned the pregnancy and asked if you've had similar experiences, share on sister/brother! What we're trying to avoid here is overt sharing when the pregnant person might behave with some difficulties or feel tender. Being reminded that they are a host for a very cute parasite may not be helpful at the moment.

- Do not ask if they are having a vaginal or C-section birth. This is creepy and wrong UNLESS they have first broached this conversation and asked for advice or any insights you have.

✳ *"Was it planned or an accident?"* No one owes you the story of a hastily convened sex session in the back of the 4WD due to ovulation happening NOW, RIGHT NOW. If they offer the story....Ok, I guess. Otherwise, let's all assume the pregnancy was due to immaculate conception and move the fuck along.

✳ ✳ ✳

Ok, we've cleared the first hurdle in NOT MENTIONING THE PREGNANCY, and now the door of conversation of being pregnant has been sprung open by your person. So let's stride through with confidence and say good things like:

"This is such happy news. I'm genuinely thrilled for you. How are you feeling?" This is a good opening as the response by your person will guide you to either continue the pregnancy convo if it's enthusiastically met or drift onto other subjects if the response is muted and low-key. Also—remember to ask about the parent when the news of the birth is shared. Most people go no further than exclaiming, "How's the baby?!?" This is the ideal time to also enquire after the health and well-being of the parent. Kids, man, they will suck the very life from you like uncooperative little vampires. Check their parents are ok—most would be happy to have some attention directed toward them and the opportunity to lie and say, "I'm doing great!" As they stand there in a four-day-old tracksuit, sipping a bucket of coffee and trying to remember what a shower even felt like.

"Wow, what amazing news! When is the baby due?" This is a good choice as you can keep it light. "Fantastic, I had my

2nd baby in spring, and I loved walking with her in the pram in the early mornings". Or it might be the catalyst to going deeper "Yeah, C-sections take all the guesswork out of the due date. My partner had her third as a C-section, and it gave us a chance to have everything ready". This gives the pregnant person an opportunity to hear about your experience and perhaps get some insight into what they'll be encountering on their journey to parenthood.

"I've heard of so many people becoming pregnant recently — it's a baby boom! Is anyone else in your circle pregnant as well?" Helpful if you want to sound them out about the level of support they have. We assume that pregnant people have an overabundance of support around them, but this is not always the case, especially with extended family members not living in the same city or even country. Even a casual acquaintance can send a text or seek someone out at a gathering to check in on them and make sure they are doing ok.

Q IS FOR QUITTING

At the end of my rowing season in May 2019, I was euphoric. I'd been part of crews that had won two gold medals at our State Masters and jagged a silver in another event. I felt strong in my mind and my body, and I adored the women in my crew. Coach Kim had preserved with me over many seasons to refine my technique and included me in crews with more precise and accomplished rowers. Unbelievably, I looked forward to the pre-dawn mornings on the river when it was quiet, watching the sunrise and moonset.

And then I quit.

Sure, there were niggles like the meniscus tear in my left knee that barked every time I squatted to pull the boat out of the water. Then there was the matter of so many of the women I adored rowing with and made the whole grind of training in the dark and the rain a laugh-fest, either pausing their own rowing career or moving overseas.

All of that could be overcome, but I knew in my heart that I needed time out of the boat to find another version of me.

I'm very resistant to change, so this was a decision not taken lightly. I knew my place in the crew would be easily filled, so that singed my ego a little. I would miss the funny asides, the feeling of a beautifully balanced boat cutting through the still body of a river, blades feathered just above the surface of the water. I'd miss being able to tell people, "Oh, when I was out on the river at 5 am this morning..." and describing myself as a rower when asked what hobbies I enjoyed.

Rowing is a very time-intensive sport. The amount of time you need to practise and train in order to be competitive in an average 3-minute and 45-second race is insane. While it is an all-over body workout, your back does get a pounding lifting heavy boats on and off gather water. And being part of a club with the commitment to attend boat and shed maintenance days as well as participate in fundraising means that for nine months of the year, rowing consumes large slabs of your life. I was curious to find out who I was without the rowing.

Turns out that I enjoyed writing and making art. I met my man-friend G. I love to walk, from Urban Nighttime Safaris to multi-day wilderness treks. I love seeing live music without taking a pass because I need to be up at 4.00 am to be at training. I get a thrill from planning a spontaneous weekend away without feeling guilty that I'm missing a regatta that we've been training for.

I think I like this version of Fiona. I may go back to rowing, but for now, I'm lining up future live music events and plotting the next wilderness walk.

You'll have your own reasons for quitting. It may be quitting on something you love deeply, but you know you have to call time to be able to free up space. Or perhaps you'll be deeply relieved quitting something you grew to hate and avoid.

Here are some good words to say if you need to hit and quit it:

"I'm sorry about this, but I'm no longer able to continue rowing/doing this volunteer role / my job". This might be all you need to say! You might not want to share your reasons beyond that or have a back-and-forth conversation about your reasons. You'll know how much to share and with who.

"I thought I had the capacity to help out / do this course / provide ongoing care. Turns out that I underestimated my other commitments, and I need to find a way to exit. Can we have a conversation about how to replace me and how I can do a handover?" Quitting often has implications for others, so don't dump and run. You want to leave people missing you rather than burning effigies. Before you tell people you're quitting, map out what tasks you'll need to hand back and when you're available to take your replacement through them. Best you have a post-quit plan in place so you're not roped into continuing in your role beyond what you feel comfortable providing.

"I see myself as someone who follows through on their commitments, so it's difficult for me to tell you that I'm no longer going forward with this project / my place in the squad / my job. I know this is probably unexpected from your perspective. Once you've had a chance to digest, can we have a talk about the next steps?" While you might have been mulling over quitting for a while, others might be shocked by your news. Respect that response, give them space and then circle back with them to do a handover / debrief. Don't be surprised if you have to keep nudging them on this. Most people are resistant to change and upheaval.

Let's quit saying things like:

"See you later, suckers!" Yesssss...sentiment might be 100% accurate, but before you torch that bridge behind you, are you absolutely confident you can handle the inevitable blowback both at the point of release and into the future?

Not saying anything at all for fear of upsetting another. You may indeed cause pain or disappointment, but you can't control the thoughts and feelings of another. Your job is to quit what your heart is no longer in and have the hard conversation To deliver that message.

"I quit." Again, the sentiment is correct, but putting some context around your decision to quit is helpful in helping others understand the decision. Understanding your reasons might mean that processes are improved, the space is made more inclusive, or people are no longer tapped to make laborious homemade morning teas for training days when perfectly delicious and ready-made food is available at any cafe. Maybe quitting and people understanding the why will improve things for others in the future.

R IS FOR RAGING

It was just after the first Covid lockdown in Sydney. I was in a telecommunications store, unravelling my incomprehensible mobile phone plan. The queue to get into the store had been long but had kept steadily moving. Numbers were capped to enter the store, so the staff were only serving a single customer at a time. Tension in the store crackled as we navigated, communicating behind masks and Perspex barriers, ensuring that we kept the 1.5-metre distance between each other. You could hear people repeating what they had said and staff leaning closer to the plastic barriers to hear muffled words. The streams of people navigating the Covid age were palpable.

The sales assistant serving me explained the options for my phone plan when an elderly man in the booth beside me exploded with anger. "I'VE ALREADY CALLED ABOUT THIS. I WAS ON HOLD FOR NEARLY TWO HOURS AND WAS TOLD TO BOOK TIME TO COME TO THE STORE. WELL, I DID THAT, I'M HERE NOW, AND YOU'RE TELLING ME THAT YOU CAN'T HELP? THIS IS STUPID AND A WASTE OF MY TIME. YOU'RE USELESS!" The young woman who was serving him dropped her head and whispered apologies.

I turned from the assistant working with me and towards the elderly man.

"What's your name?" I asked him.

"WHAT?!?" He was disarmed by the question.

"I asked what your name was. My name is Fiona," I offered.

His anger levels dropped slightly. "My name is George." He said brusquely.

"Hi George," I said simply.

There was a pause. "Hi Fiona", he replied, and the anger softened again.

"George, I get a sense that today has been pretty frustrating for you. Is that right?" I asked.

"Yes". George paused. "I need to set up a new phone contract, but I couldn't get answers on the phone. My hearing aid is not working, and because of the Covid shutdowns, I can't get it repaired quickly. I couldn't hear what they were saying on the phone." I nodded for him to continue. "I came to the store, but there are so many options, I don't know what one to pick." We looked at each other, George's anger had evaporated and been replaced with sadness. "My wife is not well, and she can't see any of her friends...." His voice trailed off, and tears filled his eyes. I continued to hold his gaze and nodded again.

"Wow, George....that sounds like a lot to deal with," I said with genuine concern. I hadn't seen my elderly parents in nearly three months. With the Covid travel restrictions in place, the isolation they were suffering was deeply troubling to me, even though the rules were designed to keep them as safe as possible while we waited for the vaccination program to ramp up. I could empathise with George's situation, and rather than see him as a ragey, cranky fella. I was instead touched by his helplessness and fear.

"George, it sounds like you're doing you're best under tough times, and I can tell how much your wife means to you." It was George's turn to nod. "I'm so sorry to hear she's unwell," I added.

"I'm sure your assistant here..." I glanced towards the sales associate who had been listening to our exchange, "...would be happy to help you with selecting the best plan for you. But just like you..." I gestured towards him, "...and me," I pointed at myself, "... she's doing her best, and it's not Ok to yell at her or get angry".

George looked at the assistant and said, "I'm sorry I yelled at you. I was frustrated. If you could help me with getting the best mob plan, I'd be very grateful." The assistant smiled and nodded and took George through the options.

I swivelled in my seat to face my own assistant. "Thank you," she said softly. "People have been really angry and on edge since some of the restrictions lifted".

"Yeah, I don't think we're very good with uncertainty and change." I agreed. "I know I get challenged by it". We smiled at each other and went back to untangling my phone contract.

I didn't do anything that day but extend some kindness to a fellow human going through a tough time. It's simple but not easy. I've had so many chances in my life to reach out and bridge the divide between another human and me. I've sometimes taken the easier option and said nothing, decided it wasn't my place to get involved or risk the chance of escalating a situation. There was no guarantee that George, in his ragey meltdown, wouldn't have socked me in the head with his soon-to-be traded-in phone, but he recognised my heartfelt attempt to make a connection and responded with openness.

If you come across a stranger or a loved one in a ragey meltdown, please check first that you're not putting yourself in danger of violence by engaging with them. I know there are a lot of nuances here, but if in doubt, step back and take care of your own well-being first.

If you have a sense that it's worth trying to diffuse the situation, try exchanging names as a way of seeing each other's humanity.

Depending on if the person in a rage is a loved one or a stranger, you might try some of these phrases:

"I can see that you're upset and frustrated. But yelling isn't helping the situation. Can you explain to me calmly what the issue is?"

"Let's take a 5-minute break as I can see this is causing a lot of angst. We can come back to this when we're both feeling calmer."

"I think it might be good to move this energy. What about a quick walk around the block to see if that helps?"

But what if you're the rage monster? How can you possibly self-soothe when the election campaign is full of vitriol from all sides of the political divide, your washing machine has shredded your favourite sweater, and the Burrito Babe has stopped serving your favourite flavour?

* * *

Well, you could try asking yourself:

"What am I really angry about here? Is that sweater that was too tight across my chest and made me all scratchy, or is it that I'm feeling weary and frighted for the planet with the upcoming election?" Uncovering really what's at the nucleus of your anger is the first step in addressing how to manage and direct the anger to be a source of action and not despair.

"Am I really angry? Or do I need a nap? A glass of water? A walk in nature? A hug from a friend?". Often anger shows up when we deny what our heart truly desires. I have a pact with my man-friend G that anytime I start sprouting devil horns, nasal hairs and a tail resembling a pitchfork. We deploy the self-care early assault package of hugs, water, banging tunes and a lie down with a book. The effect is damn near miraculous. I go from Defcon 1 in rage to a peaceful puss-cat purring happily.

"Even though I'm totally legitimate in feeling this rage, can I turn it into something useful? Perhaps a blog post that might be helpful for others? A gym session of weights interspersed with cardio? A vigorous painting session?" It's like John Lydon sang, "Anger is an energy".

S IS FOR SINGLED OUT

It was the early-1990s, and I was at a Christmas party that was attended by mainly people I went to school with while CC and the Music Factory played on the midi-system in the background. Fresh from a breakup, I was raw and felt like I was the only uncoupled person at the party. The heavy incidence of stonewashed jeans and hyper-colour T-shirts didn't help my low mood. Turns out I wasn't the only single person there…there was the Labrador that forgot to RSVP with a plus one. It was small comfort when significant times like Christmas, holidays and Valentine's Day seem to highlight society's focus on the couple to the exclusion of the single.

With us gathered around the table loaded up with 1990 food staples like cream cheese doused in sweet chilli sauce, cob loaves hollowed out and then filled with a cheese and spinach dip and bacon-wrapped asparagus, I was deflecting all questions and trying to make conversation with the Labrador.

"Fiona, I heard you recently broke up with your boyfriend". Oh fuck. That was Sharon, the fakest mean girl at our school. She had a look of mock concern on her face that I'd seen her use when she asked you if you were really going to eat that pie for lunch. Or when she made sure you were the last picked on her netball team. She deployed that same faux-sympathy while her mouth twisted at the corners with a mocking smile while you tried to run, catch and throw the netball with your gym skirt exposing your thighs, all the while tugging at your skirt to protect your body from ridicule.

She pulled Barry, her fiancé, closer to her as he leaned in for a BBQ chop from the buffet table.

"You know…one day, you'll be as happy as Barry and I." She cocked her head on the side, the poodle perm perfectly framing her smug bitch face.

Oh, this was too delicious. I turned on my best game show host smile, my face beamed and directed my gaze directly at Barry as I chirped. "Sharon, I hope for that too!" I held that million-watt smile and my laser focus on Barry as the chop in his hand went limp.

Ah, welcome schadenfreude, my old friend. I'd busted Barry's sorry naked arse at a party about nine months prior to getting a blow job from one of Sharon's close friends. I'd thrown open a bedroom door looking for Trivial Pursuit in the party house, and there was Barry, and a lady who wasn't Sharon caught mid-fellatio. It wasn't any of my business who was up in each other's business, so I'd exited the room, snapping off the light and then returning to the party to announce that Trivial Pursuit was off the games list, but what about a run to 7-11 for a Big Gulp and snacks instead? I'd never told another person about catching Barry out there with his dick in the mouth of a woman, not his fiancé, but here was my moment, and I was relishing almost as much as the lukewarm sausage rolls.

The look between Barry and I was freaking Sharon out, so she dragged him away, chopless, as I swayed happily in my moment of victory over the smug and cloyingly coupled up.

As someone who spent periods of being un-partnered, you have to endure the misconceptions and projections of other, mainly-partnered people.

From being assured that you want to throw a leg over someone else's significant other (thank you, no, I don't deal in used goods) to being high maintenance (yes, I am, the body corporate fees will blow your hair back), having too high expectations (I'm a total music snob, but everything else is pretty much negotiable) or that you're a lesbian yet to come out (no, but thanks anyway) a single person has to have a number of witty comebacks to counteract the assumptions. And look, most of the comments and projections come through a genuine curiosity of understanding the single life, especially when so much of society's norms are geared towards the couple and the creation of the family.

Fun drinking game! Next election, take a swig from your alcoholic beverage every time a politician or a media organisation references "family / friendly policies / family-first / helping families with the cost of their day-to-day bills" and so on. Truly, you'll be in an alcohol-induced coma within 45 minutes.

So I'd rather be approached with genuine curiosity rather than the assumptions, projections and put-downs. Maybe I'm in a relationship, maybe I'm not, but I've never wanted the status of being with someone to define or confine me. I don't buy into the "you complete me" claptrap. I'm a perfectly imperfect human; no other relationship status is required.

✸ ✸ ✸

Do not be a gigantic arsehole, do a single person a solid and say things like:

"God, your skin looks amazing! Let's go for a walk". See, you can do other things rather than ruminate on someone's singleness.

"Hey! What have you been up to lately?" Ask about their whole life, not just something that might be focused on their adventures in dating

"I saw Lizzo is coming to Sydney. Wanna get some tickets and make some shapes?" Ask your single friend out, ESPECIALLY if you have a partner. We can tend to lose a bunch of friends when they partner up because, I don't know, maybe they think being single is an infectious disease or likely to give you piles.

"I'm coming around on Valentine's Day to make risotto because that day is just a commercial grab for cash, and you're my forever friend". Significant dates when you're single can bite when everyone seems to be loved up, so be that self-aware friend and do what friends do and be there for each other.

"Hey, I know you mentioned that you have an event that you've been invited to with a plus one—can I be that person for you, or should we blow it off and go to a water slide park instead?" The plus one can be fraught for a single person... do you show up in all your single glory or dip out? Give your single friend some options, and make sure you take the VIP option at the water park to skip the queues and go slide crazy!

"Come around Saturday night. I'm making pie". Notice that your friend has had a string of solo Saturday nights? Get on the blower and get them round for pie and a turn at the foot

spa. No one needs to feel like they aren't worth a Saturday night because of their partnered-up status.

"I can see how much effort you're making to get out and meet people. How are you feeling?" Dating is more effort than an ultra marathon. SO MANY feelings, disappointments, naked selfies in the bathroom, texting without tone, being stood up, meeting someone that looks nothing like the profile picture, being talked at rather than too...and that's the good dates! Check in with your friend; they probably need a hydration and refuelling stop in their ultramarathon.

✸ ✸ ✸

Don't fear the single person! And don't say these things:

"There's someone out there for everyone[1]". That's not much of an endorsement with Trump having three wives, and fuck knows how many side pieces.

"It will happen when you least expect it". This is pretty much how I view urinary tract infections, so...not helpful.

"Once you stop looking, he'll turn up". Yeah, it often goes like this when you're waiting for the 288 bus into the City.

"You just have to be happy in yourself first before you can be with anyone else". Again...Trump. Shits all over your whole argument, doesn't it?

"Maybe you should get a cat?" And maybe you should go fuck yourself.

"I'm praying that the right guy comes along for you." Please, pray for something of greater significance, like the external life of Trent Reznor, our dark lord and saviour.

"You're better off alone anyway; it's not all roses when you have a partner." We've clocked that scoop, but who says that being single equals lonely? Some of my loneliest times were when I was in pretty dire couplings.

T IS FOR "THE CRIB"

Between breaking up with my fiancé when I was 29 and having my new man-friend G move in with me at the age of 49, I lived alone. And can I just say that right there were 20 years of absolute (mostly) glorious living worthy of the life promised by Mary Tyler Moore when she launched her beret into the air triumphantly in the opening credits to "Mary Tyler Moore Show"?

My very favourite thing to do as a kid was to have a sick day from school. Sure, you didn't want to be so sick you got a needle in your bare arse from the locum to stop you from vomiting so violently that you'd be a match for Linda Blair in The Exorcist. But you wanted to be sick enough that your mum fed you party pies for lunch, and you watched the Mary Tyler Moore Show as a treat.

That show was like a drug for me. Seeing a woman living her best life in a matching pantsuit, making bank, strutting about town confidently and LIVING IN HER OWN APARTMENT. Young girls in the '70s were encouraged to dream of babies and marriage, and all I could wish for was a split-level apartment in a bustling city with a kicky flip to my hair.

I got it for 20 years and when my friend Eve emerged from the initial shock of her break up with her husband confessed, "no one tells you how good living by yourself is". I nodded smugly.

No one tells you how good it is to create your own soundtrack every day without some simpleton that you cohabitate with, complaining about the "doom, dirge-fest rock" tunes you've created. You know what? I'm feeling morose because my skin is feeling dry, and I feel that Alice in Chains regally speaks to my mood, fuck-o". Few let you in on the secret that the idea of sleeping in your bed, eating breakfast in your bed and then running your business from your bed is peak living. No muppet rolling their eyes and muttering about your world basically measures 7 square metres. You can eat cheese standing up at the fridge with the door open without another malcontent yelling at you for upping the electricity bill. You can wear knickers with "Welcome to the Boom Boom Room" blazoned across the arse and a fake fur poncho without some dingbat housemate cautioning you about your sartorial choices because they have some pals around and you look like you've suffered a brain injury. You can practice callisthenics at 3 am without someone pulling the power on the stereo. You don't have to tell anyone when you're going out, where you're going or offer to get anything for anyone if you're nipping to the shops to buy crisps for dinner. Basically, living by yourself is the greatest and best secret ever kept, and if more people did it, it would lead to the complete breakdown of society as we realise that other people are completely unreasonable and bonkers, and those other people are also me.

So yeah, I'm now living with my man-friend, and I know they say that having a business is the fastest path to personal growth, but that's bullshit. A business you can sideline once the laptop snaps shut or you put your phone on silent. When you live with others, they are there, and they're relentlessly forcing you to level up and deal with your shit.

Even if you retreat into your bedroom, they stand as sentinels outside your door and leap on you to continue the house meeting or insist that you feed, water and care for them (hello, children) or want to have a 3-hour symposium on who left the toilet unflushed. Ick. Have I mentioned how divine it is to live alone?

On my path to enlightenment, i.e. living with my man friend, I've been harassed and lovingly coached through dilemmas that come up when you share the crib:

How do you divvy up the chores and tasks around the crib?

✵ ✵ ✵

Good words:

"Can we have a conversation about what needs to be done around the house so we can come up with a plan on how we both tackle the list?"

"Hey, I've noticed that I'm carrying the share of the household tasks at the moment. This is due to me getting used to having another in the house. When I'm taking on more than my fair share, can you check me on this, so we work out a fair share of the chores? But in the meantime, the cleaning of the house needs to happen. Can we tackle this together?" This is 100% me. I had to make an adjustment from dating G to living with him and the first few months of cohabitation (thanks, Covid!) I still carried on as if I was on my Han Solo. I furiously cleaned the house when he was out. I planned all the meals and recruited him to share the cooking. It was

exhausting, and I was resentful. It took G to tell me that he felt like he was an unwelcome tenant in the home we shared. G told me he wanted to pull his weight around the home, and I needed to make the shift from cute date to housemate. Holy cats, this living together thing is non-stop growth.

"I've noticed that I'm carrying the share of the household tasks at the moment. Why do you think that is?" This is a variation on the above, but it's a good way of getting the other person's insight into the situation. They may believe they are doing their fair share. Or perhaps they are distracted by things happening in their life. Or they might just need a wake-up call that they have a responsibility for the effective functioning of the household.

"This is your space, and I want you to be comfortable too. As part of that, let's chat about how we both make a contribution around the house."

"I'm struggling to keep up with my share of the chores at the moment. Can I ask for your help in taking on more of the tasks while I get through this period".

✷ ✷ ✷

Not so great words:

"Why can't you just do more around the house?" The sentiment might be correct, but on hearing this, most people would react defensively. The goal of good communication is creating positive change, and this ain't it.

"You're hopeless. Why do have I to do everything?" I get it, and I hear the frustration here but think of how this lands with the person you're delivering it to. With a better choice of words, you could achieve the goal of a fair division of labour without turning the situation nuclear.

Or...not say anything and be the silent, seething martyr. Look, the suffering saint sacrificing their peace of mind and happiness for others has aged out. There are no prizes for carrying all the load and doing all the things, especially for women that have borne the burden of managing the house and raising kids for millennia. Everyone who lives in the house has to put in, no question.

Ok, everyone seems to be contributing to housework to make the dream work, but oh-oh, somebody just cranked Cypress Hill, and I can smell the Mary J. How do we handle conversations about drug and alcohol taking in the home?

I'd get on the front foot with this and discuss very early in the house-sharing conversation where people are at with alcohol / recreational drug-taking. Is it a hard no? Only on weekends? In their room only or in shared spaces? The tricky thing with alcohol and drugs is what is an Ok amount for some will turn another into a crippling bore that eats all the waffles and spends the best part of the next day parked under the shower listening to The Door's "Break on Through To The Other Side". And no one needs that level of shit in their lives. If I was to give any guidance on drug and alcohol consumption: don't share homes with someone who partakes in the drug and alcohol life, and you're a hard no. It's not setting the scene for a relaxed home. And I know it is a narc, ma. to even mention this, but the taking of many recreational drugs is illegal. Even though you might not be imbibing, it doesn't mean the cops will look fondly at you when your next-door neighbour calls in a complaint about your home and the cops charge everyone with possession.

"I've noticed that you've been consuming more alcohol/drugs recently. What's that about?" Mention what you're seeing and ask for their feedback. Maybe something significant has changed in their life, and they're struggling. Or maybe they weren't aware that their habits had kicked up a notch.

"I know I said I was cool with you smoking weed on the weekend but it turns out I was wrong. Can we talk about how we resolve this?"

"I'm finding this hard to tell you this, but I've noticed that when you take drugs, you are much angrier and sadder. I don't think they are helping you as much as you think they do. Have you noticed this as well?"

PSA: You don't have to stay in a home where alcohol and drug consumption is happening and leading to bad or shifty behaviour. You can leave or ask the other party to. Gather in support of friends and loved ones to bolster your resolve during these times.

※ ※ ※

I'd caution against using words like:

"If you can't beat them, join them. COCAINE, HERE I COME!!!"

"You're so stupid for taking drugs/drinking excessively". I

don't think anyone that has not been held so suffocatingly tight in the grip of addiction will ever understand what it's like for someone who is. But disparaging remarks like this will just deepen the shame and make someone less likely to reach out for help out of addiction and onto the path for help.

"If you loved me, you'd stop." I wish love was enough, but when someone is an addict, it's a health issue. You can love someone and still be an addict. You can love an addict. An addict will only stop when they have decided that they have a problem and want to address it.

I mean, the world would be a lot easier if everyone was like us, but it would be fucking tedious. We need some level of tension and difference to keep it interesting and curious.

So how do we handle when one person is comfortable living with a mess, and the other wants a house as a need as a pin? Or do you like going to bed early, and the other haunts the halls well into the night? We say we're all about diversity, but how do we live with it day to day without it becoming a major issue over time?

My man-friend recommends compassionate tolerance. You're never going to meet an identical copy of you. You have to know yourself and what you're prepared to live with and overlook or have as deal-breakers. You might not love the half-drunk water cups strewn about the house but decide it's not worth making an issue over. Rather, you instead stand firm on having a fortnightly house clean no matter what so the joint is inhabitable and barnyard animals haven't taken over.

"I love my sleep, so when you come into the room and turn all the lights on to prepare for bed, it wakes me up. Can you put your pyjamas on in the other room so you don't wake me?"

We're very oblivious creatures; sometimes, you need someone to make you aware of the impact you're having on their quality of life. Small changes can yield big impacts.

Continue to work on the problem—another excellent suggestion from G, my man-friend. For example, if you're cooking one meal to satisfy the different food preferences or tolerances of housemates and you simply CAN NOT with another tofu-based meal, say so. Maybe the compromise is to share meals three times a week, and for the other four, you might cook separately or go out for meals.

"I love being able to come into a clean bathroom. For you, dropping wet towels on the floor is not a big deal for you, but can you please hang them up after your shower?" This gives context to the issue of the wet towels strewn about the floor and states your preference for a clean bathroom when you use it. By stating your needs, the other person understands your requirements and is likely to comply with the request rather than, "Hey rat-face, hang up your damn towels, or they're going over the balcony!"

Speaking of less desirable things to say:

"Why don't you just get it???" Because hot pants, we're all different and the greatest thing I ever read in the way of self-help was the phrase "Remember you're as annoying as everyone else". Sweet Georgia Brown, the TRUTH in that. Once I realised I was as agitating to others as they were to me, it opened up a world of compassion, non-judgement and the

music of Arcade Fire to me. Oh, happy day!

"If you don't stop making noise when I'm trying to sleep, I'm leaving!" I'm not saying that this is not a perfectly reasonable course of action to take, especially when it comes to the wilful interruption of blissful sleep but be sure you'll follow through on the threat; otherwise, your boundary will continue to be breached.

I don't know about you, but I'm feeling hungry. What's for dinner?

Good things to say:

"Good timing! I'm hungry too, let's look in the fridge and see what we can make"—many hands make a quick and delicious meal (old proverb). Even the smallest upright person, like a small child, can wash and dry veggies. If you're eating, you're helping!

"I'm not feeling hungry right now, but feel free to help yourself to what's in the fridge/cupboard." You're under no obligation to eat when others do. If you're not hungry, just don't use it as a continual excuse to avoid helping make meals.

"I've cooked the past few meals—can you take the running on this?" Feel like the balance is out of whack in the making of meals? Feel free to deploy the "Tip; you're it" approach.

Things guaranteed to turn your stomach:

"Get it your damn self!" I get the frustration, but unless you're in the mood for some rapid-fire snark between the parties, best avoid it.

"I'm just making enough for myself; you can do what you like." Like the one above, it might be true but try and deliver the message with less spice and more sugar.

What about the sharing of finances in a shared household? How do you navigate all the various and complex issues that people have about sharing space and money?

Money can be a festering simmer pit of disappointments, resentment and angst. With everyone's money story as unique as their music collection, small wonder money can cause the deepest of divisions. Yours, mine...ours? It's complicated 'yo.

Do you know what helped me and the man-friend feather our love-nest? Doing one of those money quizzes to determine our money archetype. Turns out I'm a worker that will work every hour God sends. I occasionally indulge in a shopping blitz to reward my hard effort. Otherwise, I doggedly stash money away in the bank that is doing sweet fuck all there. I value security, so I'm nervous about investing in the stock market. I don't feel confident (yet) in investing as I'm worried that I will lose some of my hard-earned capital. As a result, I see only minimal gains and miss out on developing a true investment strategy. The man-friend, on the other hand, is a discerner. He painstakingly researches the bejesus out of everything to ensure he has got the Best Buy or deal. While he will steadily build wealth over time, he also misses out on opportunities as he's trying to pick the best time in the market to invest to see the best returns. Understanding each other's archetypes was so helpful with our relationship and the blending of finances to maintain our home. For us, keeping our finances separate and contributing to a kitty where household expenses are drawn from works as a treat for us. While we lovingly challenge each other's safe places (my tendency to overwork / his to over research), we honour each other's separate financial goals. Even in share-house situations, it's worth doing one of these quizzes to understand the money archetypes you're living with and what attributes you can boost and how the less admirable qualities can be quarantined.

※ ※ ※

Conversations around house rules are helpful too in determining how money is applied to the expenses:

- If it's a share house and you have a guest staying over, how many nights are fair play before they trigger contributing to the household? *"I've noticed you, Margaret and Chloe have a very pleasant, no-strings-attached playroom thing happening three nights out of 7. Those extra showers—while necessary—are hitting the water bill hard. Can you cough up some more funds to pay for those shower sessions?"*

- If someone is using a particular household item like their infrared sauna for cooking their balls that chew through electricity and the other members don't as they are not woo-woo dullards, how do you reconcile this in the budget? *"It's going to take a little while for those balls of yours to deliver on the promise of an increased immune system, so while we wait for that guaranteed eventuality, can you pay for this month's electrical bill in recognition of your extra power usage?"*

- How much money does everyone contribute? When is it tipped into the kitty? When do you start selling off their PS3 to recover funds in arrears? *"So we've all agreed that $250 a month will be paid into the kitty on the first day of each month. If you're struggling with having the funds for that date, let us know. If the funds aren't in the kitty within 14 days and we're not aware of any issues, we going to have a problem and talk about you finding somewhere else to live."*

- If someone's work is insecure and their income is lumpy—are they able to contribute to the functioning of the household in other ways? *"I get that the increasing push of people into casual and unsecured work is a product of late-stage capitalism. So if you're going through a temporary slump, are you able to help out in other ways, such as ordering groceries or making meals?"*

- What is someone's idea of a good time is going to the local posh deli and dropping $80 on three items where other household members like to live like puritans and make each teabag last at least 6 cups of tea to make sure they get true value for money? *"We have different tastes and budgets. What about the kitty be used for staples only like oil, nuts, flour, milk and artisan cheese (IT'S A STAPLE—FIGHT ME!), and we use our own funds to buy our preferred menu items?"*

Let's see if we can smooth out some of the seething:

"Now that we're living together, can we have a conversation about how we pay jointly for household expenses? Do we set budgets? Or have a kitty?" Instead of having a row every time a bill drops, start as you mean to go on and have a conversation when you start cohabiting, so the mode of operation is in place from the get-go.

"We're draining the kitty before the monthly billing cycle *ends. We need to look at our joint household purchases and either see where there's some overlap or if we need to adjust our contributions"* No blame—it might be that your pet iguana's hot lamps have shot the power bill into the stratosphere. If bills are getting out of control, time to have a talk and see where the money is really being spent. There are a plethora of budgeting apps available, and they're not just useful for personal expenditure. Consider using one for tracking household bills so everyone has exposure to where the money is going and how much is left in the monthly budget before you blow a load of coin on 43 Marimekko cushions for the sunken lounge.

Let's avoid statements like:

"You're hopeless with money; you can't be trusted!" Honey,

we're all on our money journey, and some of us have a better relationship with it than others. Just because you might be all over budgeting and financial awareness doesn't mean others are. Wouldn't you get a better outcome if you offered to share non-judgemental tips on how to budget and set money goals?

"Why do you never have any money?" There could be very good reasons why money is scarce that you're not privy to. Assuming they are frittering it away or being frivolous with the expense is not kind nor helpful. Maybe they don't have the funds they said they did initially due to a change of working circumstances, redundancy or—as so many are experiencing—suffering from insecure work through limited shifts or the gig economy. Have some compassion and have a talk with them where the aim is to understand and not shame.

"I'll look after the finances. You don't need to worry about that". Financial coercion and control don't just happen in partnerships. They can also occur in share households. Reject any offers, no matter how seemingly helpful it might seem, for one party to control the finances, be the only one seeing the bills and distribute the money. Hard no. Money is freedom and choice—you deserve a say in how it's spent and saved when you're sharing spaces and lives.

U IS FOR "YOU GOT ME MATEY?"

I am shit at asking for help. I'm from a long line of women who resisted asking for assistance as it was seen as a personal failing if you couldn't be up at 4 am to milk a cow, drag the entire household's bedding out onto the verandah and beat it as it owed you money, so it was "aired", run the Electrolux through the house and make three slices, two roasts and baking tray's stacked full of veggies all because the oven was going to be switched. Not a moment's worth of that magical heat gifted by the gods could be wasted, so the oven was heaving with food. Finally, you'd scrub the linoleum floors on your hands and knees, so your knees were effectively shot by the age of 36. All of this, of course, had to be carried on without complaint.

It's no mystery that my maternal great-grandmother promptly collapsed and died after making Sunday lunch for the family. She effectively died of doing all the things. Unfortunately, that trait continued along the female line, and while I'm getting better at asking for help, a tiny part of me still feels that if I'm not doing all the things and deftly spinning many plates simultaneously, I'm somehow disappointing my great-grandmother and her shot knees from beyond the grave.

For too many years in my business, I resisted bringing in

paid employees. When I did hire people, I felt I had to prove that I was the best boss by out-working them all, so I never had to feel that I was asking them to do something that I wasn't prepared to do myself. Oh, that worked swimmingly for me right up until the point I was walking back from a HIIT class through an overgrown park in Darwin and deciding that once I returned to my hotel room, I was going to end my life. There were many reasons that brought me to that decision that day to take my life. Certainly, the inability to thrash me through overwork and not reaching out for help or delegating within my business was certainly a top-5 contributor.

After my climb out from the pit of despair, I really had to lean into asking for help. Indeed, even in the aftermath of planning to take my life, I had to ask my healthcare team for support and confess how badly I was feeling. I told friends openly and honestly that I had to be doing less than great. I started to look forward to small things like a row in the sunshine or sharing a meal. I had to look my dad squarely in the face while gripping the ledge of the kitchen bench to prevent myself from fleeing and tell him that I would not take my life and leave my nieces without their Aunty.

Other asks were not as emotionally charged. I told potential suitors that I chose not to drink wine during the week, and thank you, yes, I'm certain I'll have sparkling water with lime, please. I asked my regular cafe for two, not one marshmallow with my hot chocolate, because that pleases me so. I requested that people not stand so close in the deli queue, and this was before Covid! I live in Australia, and we're a wide brown country, and we can afford to spread out y'all! We don't need to be jammed up in each other's pits if it gets you closer to the salami selection. Spread out, and you'll get to the top of the cheese queue before you know it.

What I want you to know if you have to struggle against doing all the things yourself because people are a bit clueless, or you feel you could do it best or that asking for help is a sign of weakness is this: the doing of life goes better with help from others. The collective is a natural form of lubrication to smooth all the bumpiness of life.

So if you're struggling, here is an exercise that helps muscle with these requests:

"I'm not doing so great. Are you available for a walk sometime soon?"

"Can you pick up the ingredients for tonight's dinner? I'm slammed, and some assistance you'll be great." Don't be shy about telling others explicitly the help you need! It cuts out any confusion on others trying to figure out how best to help.

"So with this project, are you able to take it on with your current workload, or will you need to look to spread the tasks further amongst the team?"

"If I could have some quiet time on my own, that would be appreciated." Asking for time from others is totally ok, especially if you feel you identify with the traits of an introvert and need time away from people to recharge and re-group. It's helpful to let your loved ones know you're consciously taking some out, so they're not worried about you being MIA.

"I'm fine now, but can you check in on me in a few days' time to

see if that's still the case?" Don't revert to set and forget. It's totally acceptable to ask for check-in in a few days if you're feeling fragile.

"So you're welcome to come around for dinner. How about we cook when you get here, so neither of us has to worry about making something beforehand?" I don't know if your friends are like mine, but we love getting together and bringing eskies full of food that we see us fat and happy for days. What if you took the pressure to make something beforehand off the table and instead enjoyed the process of cooking together once you came together? Tacos, incidentally the world's greatest food, are perfect for group meal making, as are pizzas, salads, grazing plates of fresh vegetables, dips and cheeses.

"I'm moving house next week. Are you available to help between 1 pm–3 pm with unpacking boxes?" We all know weekends are sacred times to commune with Lord Trent Reznor and break bread at the local pub, so we can be really resistant to asking for help from friends. But if you need a hand, ask and add a time window in so that they know how long the commitment is for. You'll feel great as you know you won't be tying them up for their entire weekend. And they're stoked as they can be of help without missing out on the Bratwurst Festival that they so badly wanted to get along to.

I've got to make a tough call this weekend to let my ex know I don't want to stay in touch anymore. Can you come around, so I stay the course and either don't make the call or soften the message?"

✴ ✴ ✴

New to the asking for help stuff? Let's avoid:

Not saying anything at all. I think we can all agree that it's not helpful. Life is better with other people sharing the load. Even U2 sang about it in "One".[9]

> *One love, one blood*
> *One life, you got to do what you should*
> *One life with each other*
> *Sisters, brothers*
> *One life, but we're not the same*
> *We get to carry each other, carry each other*
> *One*
> *One*

"I hate to ask but"...as excruciating as it might feel, please don't lead with the dread of asking for help. By doing this, you're telling others that asking for assistance is a bad and painful thing. Asking for help is a good and smart thing to do. It reminds us that we're all part of the community that looks out for one another and steps in to lend a hand as needed.

"I'll do X for you if you do Y for me". I know the mutual help-out session is beneficial but practise asking for help with no expectation that you need to return that favour. If you slip into this habit, you might only ask for help if you can help another. That massively reduces the opportunity to get assistance when you need it. Of course, don't be that arsenate that taps the goodwill of others without also returning that same kindness. I trust you to know when your generosity reservoir is running low and when you need to top it up by checking in with your loved ones to see if someone needs a hand.

V IS FOR VICTORIES...AND THE HUMBLEBRAG

My friend Amber is permanently awesome. Sure, she has things that go tits up. She endures disappointments, and she still has to deal with maddening phone tree loops just to do a change of address like the rest of us, but she remains, at all times, awesome.

I tripped over Amber's awesomeness when she joined the North Shore Rowing Club. Being a much-maligned bow-sider, I barely registered any interest when this tall drink of water loomed out of the pre-dawn gloom and introduced herself as another bow-sider that had just joined the club. Coach Kim frogmarched Amber straight to seven-seat in the eighth as she was the obvious choice to take the hardest seat in the boat. Sitting in a seven-seat, your priority is to back up stroke no matter what weird jazz-like syncopated rhythm she sets down, panting out words of encouragement between each deep breath. Seven-seats are the gatekeeper between the rest of the malcontents in the boat. "What's the stoke rate (who cares, just row it, fuck you) / we're down on bow side (then introduce yourself to the tap down) / my butt hurts (I'm going to stab you with a size ten spanner as soon as I get back in the landing)" and stroke, who's only job is to set the stroke rate in the boat and remain untroubled by the riot that has broken out behind 7. Seven seats can also take the stats on the boat that gauges meters cleared per second and stroke rate and feeds that back to stroke and the cox. Oh yeah, between all this paperwork and admin, seven also rows. With this lengthy job description, Amber was our gold class standard seven-seat.

It's not enough that Amber handled all this bureaucracy with a deft inside hand. She also managed to represent the state for many years in the annual Australian Rowing Championships. Layer on top of this her natural ability to be a long-distance cyclist, a netballer, a basketballer, all the while wrangling spreadsheets and keeping a weathered eye on a company's finances in her role as a CFO.

I know. Amber is covered with awesomeness.

Racing in a squad, you get moved around a lot to row in different boats and with interchangeable rowers based on availability and age class. You can go from easily nailing a race one week to catching crabs, having zero leg drive and limping across the line stone-motherless-last in the next.

One of my more heartbreaking races was a 1400m on our home course. We'd done solid training, I'd eaten all the right foods in the lead-up, and the body was warmed up and fully flexed. I was in the second crew, Amber in the first. On the start line, our boats lined up amongst a field of five. With the starters siren, we launched into our racing sequence designed to get the boat up, sitting high in the water and achieve race pace quickly. Even in the start phase of the first 25 strokes, I knew we were off our game. I was in seven-seat myself, and I struggled to back up the stroke effectively. The leg drive was lacklustre. Catches were limp, and the finishes were…feeble. Our cox tried everything to help us lift. Words of encouragement, bribery, sledging, all to no end. It wasn't our day. One boat after another glided by us with ease. Finally, the tortured row was over. We'd come forth out of 5 boats. The sombre mood in the boat was lifted when we realised that our First Crew held off a fast-finishing Sydney Uni crew can claim the win.

Back on the jetty, our crew pulled in the boat and made our way to congratulate our winning squad members. Barbara, from the winning first crew, said to us, "Hey, I really saw you coming back at the end of challenge Mosman".

Honey, no. You were so far down the course ahead of us that you'd moved into another suburb. We'd staggered across the line, beat and bad-tempered while you'd won the race, paused for photos, made cocktails and were filing your nails. I know what Barbara was doing, she was trying to make us feel better from the sting of a bad row, but it was actually making the loss that much greater by inventing a scene that had never played out. We weren't coming back to Mosman. Mosman spanked us like a night at the Hellfire Club.

I was gathering my things, ready to depart the club, when Amber moved across.

"How was the row?" She inquired, absently tucking the winning medal out of my view.

"It was...fucked." I admitted. "We couldn't get the leg drive going, there was no run on the boat, and it was just a slog".

Amber considered this. There was silence between us while we let the moment hold. She'd won. I'd lost badly. But in that exchange, Amber gave me space to let me tell her how it was. She didn't attempt to placate me, jolly me along or try on some trite "next time will be better" claptrap. Amber gave me a great gift that day. She was strong enough to know she could handle my honesty without rushing to make me feel better, but more importantly, she knew I was strong enough to bear the disappointing loss without letting it drag on me.

"That sucks. I'm sorry." Amber said quietly. And then: "So," Amber said, a slow smile creeping across her face. "Want to go get second breakfast?"

I nodded and grinned, knowing a caramel slice as a second breakfast was going to take the edge off the bitter taste of disappointment.

Amber, in all her winning awesomeness, really stood out for me that day and many days since. I've never felt diminished in her company or "lesser than" when her crew did so better than the one I competed in. She's curious about you, what you think and what your experience was. In times when she could bask solely in her own awesomeness, she's bringing people in closer, not holding them at a distance, asking about them, checking in and amplifying others' efforts.

Couldn't we all do with a little more Amber in our lives, people who are interested in us and who elevate rather than flatten our spirits? We all wish for those stand-out days or moments, and Amber has had plenty in rowing, but it's the way she brings forward everyone else in her wake and makes us feel pretty amazing is a superpower.

Doing great, thanks, but self-aware enough to know that others might be having a shit time?

Try these on for size:

"What's going on with you, matey?"

"How was that (experience) for you?"

"Can you tell me more?"

"When you say things have been shit lately....can you tell me a bit more about that?"

"What's new with you, love?"

"I'd love to hear more about you and what's going on in your life?"

"I'm sorry...that sounds like a lot to deal with. I'm here for you right now if you'd like to tell me more"

✹ ✹ ✹

For the love of all things cheesecake, please avoid these self-serving phrases:

"You know, this reminds me of a time when I overcame the challenges I was facing by using essential oils / activated almonds/scream therapy". None of these are bad suggestions... but avoid turning the conversation to your triumph over the trials you've faced. Unless your friend asks if you've been through something similar, and in that case, let 'er rip!

"This too shall pass". Not all things pass. Dead's dead, for example.

"One day, you'll look back at this and realise how far you've come". That might be one day, but it's not today, knock that Smiley McFakey shit off.

"I faced similar stuff...but look how happy I am now!" You might be happy, but you're also being a smug dickhead.

"Sorry to hear that...hey, wanna see my medal / my award, my post about my kid getting an A on the clarinet exam?" Susan, no one cares about your idiot kid, and that clarinet can get jammed up his arse for all the empathy you're displaying right now

"Awwww...is it really as bad as you think?!?" Dunno...but maybe while I figure that out, I can peel the skin from your unhelpful face?

"Well, you have to take the good with the bad!" No, I just seem to have to be surrounded by shit-for-brains that make a rubbish experience that much worse.

W IS FOR WORKPLACE

The concept of making a meaningful contribution within a company (or even a company of one!) and being financially compensated for it, of course, is a fucking revelation to the British Royal Family, Donald Trump and his band of charmless grifters, trust fund man-babies and Kid Rock. Yes, we're talking about all things workplace.

The workplace throws up so many "say what, homie?!?" dilemmas. Let us turn our attention to the space we spend the bulk of our time outside our homes.

I have the dream job for introverts. I have an awesome team of Divas employed to do the lord's work in construction and fit-out. They have offices they can attend, or they're able to work from their home, their car, on the back of utes, on planes or in cafes. Before Covid swept through workplaces and proved that many typically office jobs could be worked from damn-near anywhere and not tied to the antiquated 9 – 5 cubical life, Diva was set up so we could work from wherever. We have had a head office in Sydney for the past five years. I doubt I would have visited more than a dozen times, and at least half of those would have been for chowing down on the best peri-peri chicken sandwich known to humankind at the cafe downstairs. I get to spend the bulk of my workdays when not travelling interstates, being on-site or visiting clients working from home wearing activewear and listening to playlists dominated by Trent Reznor and Amyl and the Sniffers.

Even being liberated from the cubicle nation still means that workplace issues come up that need a deft touch. Especially with people working out of the office, you need to think about what needs to be communicated and how issues need to be tackled. How do you get a face-to-face meeting to tackle delicate issues when your team is working on dining tables and converted closets? Is delivering hard-to-hear messages ok via email or the slack channel?

Many issues and many workplaces are mired in confusion and what to say. Let us gather around the photocopier and see if we can't choose good words that reinforce the boundary with a work colleague or have a difficult conversation when the first impulse would be to hurl a leg of ham at their insufferable face.

1. When you need to tell a colleague, "I can't do that", and set a boundary

One of the more common complaints in the workplace is the trampling of boundaries or the willful ignorance of them even being necessary. From the overshare to the "hey-ho, it's all a bit of a laff" sex pests, to the unrealistic workloads employees are saddled with, to refusing to move with times and offer flexible working… it's a shit show. No wonder employees are refusing to return to the workplace in droves. Given a chance, wouldn't you want to avoid Les and his undermining of you to your manager? Of course, you'd rather work from home in your sweat pants with "Welcome to the Boom Boom Room" stencilled across the arse.

Say you're faced with yet another all-caps URGENT demand to drop everything and DEAL WITH THIS NOW. NOW. NOW, DAMN IT. Oddly, this can be a scenario that works in your favour, as this type of outrageous demand is usually from a repeat offender. You can calmly respond with, "I have a number of time-critical tasks right now. Which one do you suggest I postpone to work on your request?" This smelly-eyed assessment should pull up the Berk-making demands. The onus is now on THEM to come up with a decision—and the accountability that comes with that—regarding what project gets jettisoned in favour of theirs.

Another approach you can try is "I wish I could add this to my list, but I can't accommodate that task within my current workload". This is stellar because it offers no gaps for negotiation. It's a no dude. Tell your story, walking. Repeat offenders often vaporise when you stand up to them and assert a boundary. They are used to people just wanting to be rid of them, so they begrudgingly agree to their unreasonable demands. Much like irksome vampires, once you invite them to sample the fruits of your agreeable nature, they will exploit it like a hyperventilating oil executive seeing pristine wilderness for the first time.

Another common boundary bozo announces themselves when you gather your bags and make for the door to collect kids, make the 4.12 express, attend a cheesemaking class or skive off to a medical appointment. You're met with a smarmy "oh....leaving early today, are we?!" To which the only response needs to be, "I'm operating on Universal Time. So I've actually worked late". If you don't think you can carry off this flippant response with a straight face, by all means, meet the smarm with a bright smile and say, "I am! And I'm really happy with the work I pumped out today!" Feel free to add in an enthusiastic thumbs up at this point, too.

Got that office numb-nuts that dump all the work on you that offers no glory while they get to showboat and preen under the appreciation of the management team? Perhaps you're fed up with being passed over for promotion, or you need to stick firmly to your hours in the office so you can do the kid run without blowing through every red light to pick them up before childcare closes.

"I've got a full plate right now, and I'm not able to help at this time".

"No"—still and always a complete sentence.

"I've got a hard stop at 3 pm today when I need to leave the office. I can help until this time, and then you'll need to finish off the project or find someone else to assist.

Avoid:

"Maybe if you can't find anyone else to help, I can try and find some time...." A whole lot of breaches in those boundaries. Stand firm, either you can or you can't and be at peace with that decision. If you coach your responses with "maybe's", "try", "might", and "perhaps", you open a door of opportunity for the person making the request to edge open that they will stride through again and again, so you fold and just do the damn thing. Your own priorities, peace of mind and goals matter. Don't elevate every request ahead of your own to-do's.

"I can't help this time, but I will next round" Who's to say that you might not be even more overwhelmed than you are now? Let each request stand on its own merits. You're under no obligation to make future commitments to soften the inability to help out this time.

"I'm really busy right now, but I'll do this overnight". You're fine to stick to your work hours. The modern workplace demands so much of us, so regular breaks and rest periods are non-negotiable. As the owner of a business, I do work after hours but do so as it allows me downtime during the day to go for a massage, a Pilates reformer class or have some quiet time to tackle business strategy. I have a company policy where repeated after-hours work is not encouraged or expected. We need some chill time, so we show up as our best selves during our work days.

2. When you need to ask for something at work—more time off, more help, more money, etc

Good/great things to say:

"I'd like to help out get my parents set up with in-home aged care on Wednesday next week. Can my work schedule be adjusted for this?" Notice around time off is GOLD to an employer or management. It allows for meetings to be rescheduled or for clients to be told about a change of deliverables. There'll be some times when forward notice is not practical or possible so where you can, give the heads up.

"I'm finding that my workload is really heavy at the moment. Can you take some time to work with me through the priority tasks and see what can either be re-assigned or delayed?" Cascading projects with slipping timelines can mean that a well-planned week looks like the aftermath of a natural disaster within hours. Within Diva, we find it helpful to ask another to set aside 15 mins or so to work through the task list, so it gets it straight in the head like a whirlpool of to-dos. We look at what can be reallocated or ask the client for added time. Another helpful thing to do is look at the task and ask the most obvious question—does this even need to be done by me?

Maybe another Diva has done something similar that we can reshape for this task. Recently, a Diva Simone needed some examples of our past Queensland work to show a client. Instead of creating a whole new stack of portfolio pages, Sue spoke to me in the passing of this request, and I told her that I'd done something similar recently that I could send straight across. Winning!

"I'd like a wage review, please. I've looked into comparable roles in the industry for context. I feel that I've added a lot of value to the business recently, and I'd like to discuss my remuneration" Diva Georgia recently raised the prospect of a wage increase in her annual performance meeting, and I was pleased to see it. Especially if you're female, ask for that wage review. All the data shows that women are paid less than their male counterparts in comparable roles, and it's up to the employees and management to ensure that the gap is erased. You might not always get the wage increase you are after, but it's great to signal your ambition to your bosses and know you're advocating for your worth.

Less good things to say:

"I know I wasn't in yesterday, and I would have called, but I got busy at the vet's" Important and vital stuff will come up regularly during work hours. Modern times mean you can reach your immediate supervisor through text/email/calls via any number of platforms. There's no excuse not to let people know why you are MIA today. Put people in the picture, and don't be a disappearing act; otherwise, you'll be disappearing right out the door in time.

"I'm not going to help with that". The sentiment might be correct. It's the delivery that's missing a beat. You'll need help at some point in your job, so don't mark yourself as an unhelpful git that only looks at you for themselves.

"When do I get my pay rise?" Points for chutzpah, but the obvious answer is, "how about never?" You need to properly frame conversations around wage rises to signal your intent and give the business time to review and look at what they can offer. Set yourself up for success by having your reasoning and research rock solid.

3. When a new team member joins the company, you want to give them time to get acclimated but also introduce yourself and let them know who you are and what you do.

This is really pertinent to my situation right now. I'm introducing new members to the team and with us working remotely or on-site. I'm working out the best ways for the new Divas to feel part of the team when there's no requirement to turn up to a singular workplace every day. The traditional format of a workplace where everyone turns up and works to the same-ish hours is an express route to feeling part of new work culture and getting to know who's who in the zoo. With decentralised working now the norm, I'm using some of these good words to help new requires to feel Diva-ish:

"We're going to have an all-team conference call so we can meet our new team member. On the call, I'd love for you to introduce yourself, what your role is and what's the one tip you'd like to share about working in Diva that would be helpful to our new recruit?" I'm digging this as, firstly, I'm rubbish with names, but if you team an introduction with something memorable like a tip or insider knowledge, they are more likely to remember it. I also like the idea of asking for suggestions and tips. People love to be helpful and want to share their past experiences so others can learn from them.

Asking for advice from the new hire also aids the newbie in knowing where to go for advice. For example, Diva Louise shared some IT hacks on the welcome call. So next time a Divas computer is on the fritz, and they're about to jettison the computer off the balcony, they know who to go to first.

"How do we set you up for success? How do you like to structure your day?" Rather than be surprised that your new hire likes to batch answering their emails, so it seems that they are silent for large slabs of time, ask up about how they like to work. Many times this won't be possible when shit goes bad, and everyone needs to be all hands-on to meet deadlines or to cover for someone who needs to collect a sick child. But it's instructive to have that visibility around their idea workflow and habits. The Divas know not to call me between noon and 1 pm as I'm most likely dining on pie, salad and Coke Zero for lunch and taking a hot minute to EXHALE. When you've been thinking and working all things Diva since 7 am, you need a hot minute to nourish yourself and stare out to the middle distance before you launch yourself back into the maelstrom.

"If you need some direction or need to ask about something, how about gathering your queries together, and we'll go through them at 10 am and 3 pm each day?' This is super helpful for both parties. The new requirement doesn't avoid asking for help because they don't want to be the annoying person with so many questions. And for the manager or supervisor knows they won't be interrupted constantly. Structured question and answer time is neatly folded into the day.

I'm going to avoid this:

"If you need anything, sing out!" What is "anything"? How often can I ask for help? If I can't get a hold of you, who else can I turn to? Vague offers like this do no one any favours. Be explicit in who, what and where.

"It will all be there in the onboarding document." The standard operating procedures (SOPs) should be a living and evolving document added to when gaps in the information are identified. SOPs are not exhaustive and absolute, no matter how much you add to them. There are always nuances and sidebars that you can add to broaden their comprehension.

"Don't bother me. I'm busy". I may not sound as brusque as this, but I know that's the vibe I can give off at times when I'm consumed by my own work. If I'm the leader of Diva, I need to embody that role and not brush off team members because I'm too busy to help. No new hire enjoys feeling isolated and sidelined. It's up to the manager and team members to help them feel as welcome as possible and jazzed to feel part of a team.

What NOT to say to women in the workplace.

This broad topic needs more words than I care to devote to it when a counter meal is on the other side of this chapter. Suffice to say, what I don't cover here, please make haste to your nearest female and ask them: "What's best to avoid saying to a female in the workplace". Prepare yourself to have the woman throw back her head, emit a delighted cackle and sit you down to get schooled.

This by no means is an exhaustive list, but the ones that women commonly reference when we hold our monthly lodge meetings based on the rolling theme of "How to destroy the patriarchy and other cream cake recipes". What fun!

"Oh, are you leaving early to pick up the kids again?" No, I'm leaving early to plot your untimely demise when you accidentally impale yourself on a pitchfork while reading the sports pages and avoiding the work-in-progress meeting.

"Can you organise the office gift for the departing colleague / new baby/birthday celebration?" This chore—and make no mistake, it is a chore—regularly falls to the females in the workplace. Can't a salute and stapler from the stationary cupboard suffice instead? If you're male and reading this, next time, volunteer yourself to be the one to marshal the troops and chase them down for money.

"Make me a coffee while you're up." Make plans for your balls to be kicked through the roof of your mouth, fuck-o.

"Can you take the minutes for this meeting?" If you're the one saying this and there's a near-equal mix of men and women in the meeting, ask yourself why you're directing this request to a female and not a male. This tedious task of taking notes that fuck all people read afterwards has been the burden of women for too long. How about we all take our own notes and agree on a set of follow-up tasks at the completion of the meeting? And then we behave like the professionals we are and hold ourselves accountable to the action list without expecting the females to politely follow up?

"You're too sensitive/emotional/take things to heart". It's called being a human, and sometimes humans are in pain, and we cry. Be advised, that when you leave the workplace there will be nothing but tears of joy and month-long celebrations in the cafe toasting that your entitled and insufferable arse is no longer haunting these halls.

"You just need to learn to toughen up. I didn't get to where I am by avoiding constructive criticism of my performance"

No, you got to where you are by the patriarchal power systems upholding and rewarding the mediocre and mildly talented. Not everyone was born with your privilege, and the path made smooth to each new income and management level. Some have had to, you know, sweat for it. And even then, they are largely locked out and overlooked for positions of power like prime ministers, presidents, CEOs, managing directors, popes and board members.

"You know, when I hugged you, I only meant it as a concerned friend." Friends respect boundaries and understand that workplaces come with a different set of behaviours and rules. If a female has a preference for no hugs, respect that and if you have a problem with that and feel like your friendly hugs are being misconstrued, then yes, you're the arsehole.

"I'd love to ask you out on a date". This is fraught, I know. So many people meet their partners through the workplace, and it's been a very fruitful hunting ground. But the workplace evolves. Once upon a time, if you wanted to make a sale using a credit card, you used to place the card in a metal contraption, line up a payment slip in triplicate over the top and brace yourself again on a firm surface to perform a movement similar to the upright row to impress the card onto the triplicate slip. Even then, you had to fill in all the details on the subsequent sheets as the triplicate carbon was never enough to make clear the total cost. AND—you even had to call up a national hotline to get authorisation for bill amounts greater than $100. I mean, if we can evolve from that time-consuming malarkey we can also check ourselves to make sure we really want to pursue a partner in the workplace. Power imbalances, company policies prohibiting relationships between employees and the general discomfort from other team members while you lock eyes with your paramour over the mechanic's engine bay should give you pause for thought. Is pursuing a relationship about tasting the forbidden fruit and having a bit of fun, or is it something deep and long-lasting? Your honest answers to that should help guide you on either making a choice to seek work elsewhere, to pursue this relationship or look for happy hunting grounds elsewhere and leave this dalliance as a bullet dodged.

X IS FOR X RATED

Ah great. Straight from the workplace into three in the bed and how to ask for some post-sex care...LET'S GET IT ON!!!

My entry into sexual education was brilliant and highly recommended. It involved a "Where did I come from" illustrated book, a cringeworthy "information night" as an 11-year-old in the school library, chaperoned by my Mum, who was bent out of shape for missing "Porridge" in the telly and best of all—through Music videos.

Australia has this great public broadcaster who, on a Friday and Saturday night at station close, became "Rage", where music videos ran back to back until mid-morning the following day. Think MTV without the annoying presenters that set your teeth on edge. Just get to the music, fuck you!

You could be adjusting your perm before you went out on the tiles with Rage cranking in the background showing "Beat It", "Sweet Child O'mine", and "That Ain't Bad". Then when you slinked in the door as dawn was breaking with an ill-advised kebab in your hand, you flicked on the telly, collapsed on the futon and settled in from more music video goodness from Bronski Beat, Yothu Yindi and Kylie Minogue. Good times!

The best nights were when you stayed at home and Rage showcased the banned videos, and that's when the illustrated picture books gave way to Madonna moaning and writhing her way through a hotel corridor in "Justify My Love". Or, the very obscure but visually striking "Imagination" by Belouis Some. It had a long-form X-rated version of a bored woman sitting topless at dining tables while the male vocalist marched through the scene, framed by two identical backup singers. Sure, why not? And then there was "Girls on Film" from Duran Duran, where you had gorgeous women in glomesh tops dancing in a boxing ring while a guy in a gimp mask looked on impassively. It was the perfect combination of sex and music, and I didn't understand most of what I was watching. The takeaway for me was that sex needed a soundtrack, and Madonna was an absolute baller when it came to teaching her target audience of young women and gay men to claim pleasure on their own terms.

Those that are judging modern Madonna for her facial enhancements and the latest younger lover seemed to have missed the part that before Madonna, sex-positive role models were pretty thin on the ground. She released a book called "Sex" that explored her fantasies. She sang songs about self-pleasure and being both the dominator and the submissive. It was a smorgasbord of sex, and Madonna was the head chef.

I wish I'd learned to advocate for my sexual needs when I was younger. Even with Madonna's brash assertiveness to "Express Yourself", there was a lingering stigma that women's pleasure was secondary to their male partners. Case in point. I once asked a group of girlfriends around mid-age what the balance was with oral sex: did they give more than they received? Resolutely, the answer was GIVE and overwhelmingly so—as low as maybe 1 in 10 as an average. There were a bunch of reasons for this. Many men thought the Clitoris was a Greek Island. Women got fed up with asking for oral sex and decided to take up scrapbooking instead. And that men prioritised their own sexual pleasure, so once they climaxed, it was time for sleep or the change a TV channel. HOT!

※ ※ ※

Let's change that up, shall we? Here are some good words I'd encourage you to use when in sexual congress with another.

"Tell me what you like." I hadn't had many sexual partners, but when J asked me this when we became lovers, I KNEW it was significant. I was 21, and before anything had ever happened, the dude had just blown my mind. It's VERY HOT to ask what the other party likes and enjoys. Just because you've had some experience in the sack means that you're a sexual demon, is like thinking that because you once bought some cask wine to a BBQ means that you're now a sommelier. Treat yourself to the joy of getting to know another sexually. This is where the beginner's mindset really pays dividends.

"I'm not feeling like sex tonight. Can we cuddle/hold hands/have a shower/massage my shoulders instead" You are under no obligation to have sex if you don't feel like it. No marital status, how many clothes you have on, what sexual acts you might have performed or how much money was sunk on a candlelit meal—you are never under any obligation to have any sort of sex or continue with a sex session. You can decide no more, or you might want to instead state what you'd prefer—like kissing, sleep or just some alone time to do skin care. Having sex with someone who is not an enthusiastic participant is pretty rank. Respect the no / no now / not like that, thanks.

"I'd love to talk about exploring so other ways we can enjoy ourselves sexually. Are you open to chatting further about this?" Not all conversations about sex are best to take place when you're butt naked and things are moving at a steady clip. It's a pretty vulnerable state you find yourself in. If you layer this with talking about your sexual needs—it's not the ideal forum. Consider having conversations outside the bed where the performance pressure is cooled and desires aren't heightened. I highly recommend having deep and meaningful conversations about the deep and meaningful on public transport. You've got a captive audience, and fuck knows everyone is bored to the tits listening to someone's endless EDM playlist through a Smart Phone. We all could do with some hot talk about your sexual preferences and/or hang-ups. Please, do go on. Jokes aside—talk about sex outside the boudoir. Pre-planning really pays dividends in this case.

※ ※ ※

Want the sexy times to evaporate? Avoid these:

"I wish you were better at foreplay. Anthony, the boyfriend I had when I was in Brisbane, was fully sick at it". Do not compare your current paramour with previous ones. Especially while engaging in sex acts. Firstly, it's demeaning, and secondly, if he was that good at sex, why are you no longer with his hot arse?

Disrespecting people's boundaries or pushing them to go further than they feel comfortable. This might sound like, *"Oh come on, you liked doing this last time"*, or *"But we're already naked and turned on...let's just try for a few more minutes.*

You'll get into it." The sex session might be hotter than the surface of the sun, but once you've heard your partner say no more, heed that call.

"Why don't you want to try (insert sex act—haw haw haw)? My boyfriends have all loved it when I do this with the" One person's pleasure is another's peeve. One person's signature sex act is another's "fuck, no!" Aren't humans so gloriously contrary and hard to figure out? Maybe your partner may want to try what you enjoy so much in the future. Maybe they won't. But in the meantime, isn't it fun to explore what works for you both, and you might even discover some new ways to blow your tiny mind.

Y IS FOR YOUNG FOLK

I don't know about you, but my bingo card for 2021 did not include "War in Western Europe". We're all so fatigued and emotionally barren after the past two years of the pandemic. The hope was that we could transition into 2022 with some time and space to replenish the last nerve we were running on. A bare-chested, bear-wrestling (I'm Team Bear, by the way) megalomaniac soon put paid to that fairy tale. And while I'm on the subject, the decade that kicked off in 2020 sure does suck. I hope it's some goodness is about to break through, especially for those that have lost people they love and homes that they have built due to the pandemic, natural disasters and theatres of war.

If you're struggling to process all this pain and upheaval, imagine how our young people feel. For many, their critical first few years of school were spent tethered to the dining table, away from friends and a structured learning curriculum, while the race was on to first develop a vaccine and then roll it out, so people had a chance to live alongside COVID. Other deeply unlucky kids faced the reality of daily air raid sirens warning them of oncoming missiles and taking cover. Even unluckier kids didn't even get an early warning and instead had to be dragged through obliterated buildings and crumpled stairwells to safety, and taking a chance on the cruel refugee roulette system where you might find yourself in a new country or jammed up for years in a tent city on a countries border. Children in many parts of the world face drought, spending hours where they should be learning in school and seeking water from dried-up wells under the searing heat. In Australia, kids have seen their homes, bushland and native wildlife be incinerated under unprecedented firestorms. While others have had their entire homes and possessions swallowed up by once-in-a-thousand-year storms and floods.

I don't know about you but even typing that list of catastrophic events left me heavy and emotional—can you imagine how our young people are trying to parse all this?!?

While I don't have any young people living with me, I do have two nieces I'm very close to. I've watched how their parents steer them from the most violent and troubling footage on social media and the TV and create a safe and honest space for my nieces to ask questions and get honest answers.

Like most kids, my nieces are inquisitive and curious—they want to understand the world they live in and how other people live. Their questions about war, famine, natural disasters and death don't arrive on your timeline. It's on theirs, so this means. Tricky and touchy questions happen when you're concentrating on traffic, on your last frayed nerve, distracted by a task or rushing to get them out the door. KIDS NEVER HAVE QUESTIONS WHEN YOU'RE RELAXED AND HAVE AN "OPEN FOR BUSINESS" SHINGLE HANGING OUT.

So let's get you prepped for those Qs. These suggestions will give you some starting points for opening up the conversation, rather than dismissing them and having them feel like they're wrong to have questions and that they can't come to you for the big heavy stuff.

I'm sure you're pretty much all over this as a parent or guardian, but as the first point of call, please filter the information that comes into your homes. This looks like parental controls on what can be viewed on social media and the apps. Switching off the TV, so the constant news stream is not the soundtrack to the house. Think about little ears that might be nearby when you jump on a call and lament with a friend all the terrors you see in the world.

Next up, if your young person comes to you and asks about the pandemic, a natural disaster or war, try and stop what you're doing and give them your full attention. Now is not the time for blithe or dismissive answers. You can ask them, "what have you heard?" So you know exactly what information they're working off. In the example of war, they might be fearful that war will come to their neighbourhood. If the theatre of war is far from you, you can reassure them that the war is very far away and they are not in danger. You might suggest ways you can research how you can help others that are caught up in the war. Finding ways to help—by donating money, resources, or time—can be an incredibly powerful way to feel helpless and more hopeful. If you are close to the war zone, you can acknowledge the fear and the uncertainty without the hysteria and reassure them there's a plan in place if you need to leave. Tell them that when you go, you'll go together.

Saying, "I can hear how worried you are about (fill in the blank of any unspeakable horrors that take place in the world, daily)—but I want you to know you're safe right now" is also very calming for a kid. Kids don't always have an understanding of the past and future. They are very much tied to the "now", so if you can keep them centred at this moment and reassure them that they are safe, right here and now, it will go a long way to providing reassurance and comfort.

"Can you share with me what you're scared about"—this is an illuminating question to ask as it's helpful to uncover exactly what's on your kids' minds. You might be assuming they are worried about not having their toys to play with if disaster strikes, but they might be really worried about an elderly neighbour that lives alone and what will happen to them if everyone needs to evacuate. Gather intel and then make a plan together on how you can tackle or ally those fears.

※ ※ ※

Please avoid:

There's nothing to worry about!" This might be true, but you're the only voice against so many others that might be whipping up hysteria. Acknowledge the fear, uncover what lies beneath it and then map out a plan on how to overcome it if and when it does eventuate.

"You're too young to worry about this sort of stuff". Oh, how we all wish this was true, but kids are incredibly perceptive and have access to so many forms of information, often without your filter applied. Kids can feel the tension in the home, they know when voices drop low, and doors are closed to have adult conversations, shit is going bad. It's better to acknowledge the challenges at hand and keep the lines of communication open.

"I thought I told you there was nothing to worry about". You might have calmed fears repeatedly for the past six days, most of them when you were trying to have an uninterrupted toilet break. But you need to keep on reassuring, reinforcing they are safe as often as the child needs to hear it. I can guarantee that even though they're seemingly raising concerns every hour, they are living in full-blown terror of what might happen every ticking second. That stuff is wearing on adults. It's excruciating for kids.

A final word on disasters—natural and man-made. Get out sooner than you think. Best to walk away with only your loved ones than stay past the point of no return. Everything is replaceable except the ones you love and care for.

Z IS FOR ZEALOTS

Holy Christ, the past few years of nationalism, seriously screwy fringe churches, the rise of the white wellness warrior women and the pandemic conspiracy hysteria has given rise to the Zealot. Even with a backdrop of all this upheaval and turmoil, no one asked for the march of Zealots.

Not surprisingly, social media has been a very effective broadcast channel for Zealots to spread their hysteria. So much better if they have an online course, e-book or consulting services to shill.

During the Covid lockdowns, I found a very effective means of activism. I got right into reporting these zealots for their anti-science, homophobic, racist, right-wing nut-cracker views. The best thing was that I could do it from my bed and wrapped warmly in my Jim-jams.

I'm very intrigued by how people drift from clear-headed thinking and behaviour to fundamentalism. I've finished reading Van Bodhams brilliant book Qanon and On. She cites research where one of the unifying traits that many of those seduced by conspiracy theories share is they've experienced trauma in their lives. To make meaning of that trauma, they look for answers about why their life has been touched by disaster and devastation, while others have a seemingly easier life path. Their search for answers might lead them to online groups that may have a fairly benign set of reasons. Being told that you're so strong of character you've been marked for this test of your fortitude and spirit is alluring, but it soon spirals down the rabbit hole where you're being told that your trauma is the entry portal to the Great Awakening. And because you've been through a trauma, you're especially susceptible to posts and news stories about other people—especially kids—being in pain and soon you're balls deep in Save The Children quagmire. People believe bonkers things like 30,000 kids being trafficked through underground caves in Melbourne. What—and I say this in the strongest possible terms—the fuck?

Humans don't do well with uncertainty, so in times when there's an uptick in conflicts and shifting political ideologies, people want to try and make sense of it. I can see the lure of conspiracy theories. They are like a siren song as they draw you in with a sense of community, and you feel that you're unravelling a puzzle and pulling random threads together, and bingo-bango, you now see what you've previously been blind to. People across the world are being held in thrall by companies and individuals who have a vested interest in turning you away from the true crises of our time like gun control and climate change.

✶ ✶ ✶

What can you do if you're being targeted by a zealot trying to draw you into their sticky web of all-caps rage and breathless, harried conversations about the end of days, how you had an implant of 5G in place of a vaccine or that God Hates Gays? (For once and for all, this is demonstrably wrong. God loves gays, and that's why he's given us the joyous celebration of life that is Queer Eye, Dykes on Bikes and disco music).

"This is not a conversation I'm prepared to have with you". There's no debating with zealots. They just double down on the crazy. In Qanon and On, Van speaks with therapists and experts in the reprogramming of cult-like conspiracies, and the advice is to stay well away from debating the ideology. Instead, stay engaged with them and have conversations based on shared interests or experiences that you enjoy doing together, such as bush walks or art classes. A neutral and non-judgmental approach will help those loved ones who are ready to emerge from the Zealot haze to find support on the other side.

"I know you hold those beliefs as true, but I have a very different viewpoint. For the sake of our relationship, we need to find other things to discuss" It's not your job to change someone else's mind, especially when they hold so firm to their ideology. Only when someone is ready to emerge from the conspiracy haze is there any chance of having a reasonable discourse with them.

"I know you feel this e-course/seminar/online program would help me understand your beliefs better. To be honest, they are not something I'd find useful or of interest. Please don't ask me again." The Amway model of pestering your friends to buy your shitty products lives on with the conspiracy pushers. It's now expanded to sell natural protocols to rid yourself of the vaccine, learning to protect yourself from the chemical trails the government is running covertly and NFI e-courses that sell artworks that look like they have been created in clip-art.

These phases might be so very good to say (much like a bag of potato chips taste so good for dinner but ultimately does not satiate you), but you could end up in the Town called Regret:

"NUTTTTTTERRRRRR!!"—So very satisfying but ultimately not helpful if you want to still maintain a relationship with your loved one. They are going to lean in harder to their unhinged beliefs, and you're creating further distance between you that might be too far to bridge if and when they decide their conspiracy theories don't hold much water.

"Are you a little bit fucked in the head?". See above.

"That's nothing. Have you heard about the Illuminati and the people who are actually lizards that control the world?!?" Please, don't feed the bears. But then again, I look at the band of Trumps and their acolytes, and I think, you know, there may be something in this theory.

"All of that has been debunked, you know." True. But people who believe in extreme ideologies feel they have done their research and uncovered information that supports their extreme views. Any counter research you provide will be dismissed. No one wants to feel stupid as they'll fire back with their own list of sketchy sources that support their extreme views.

"I thought I knew you." If you want to keep the door open to a future with your loved one, the advice is to be as non-judgmental as you're able to be. When the rabbit hole spits them out, they are going to need bonds with others to rebuild from.

TL:DR

Need a quick fix of good words to say when you're tits deep in a sticky situation? I got you, hot stuff.

The guard rails:

- Try to avoid important conversations when tempers are frayed, and the antagonism is sitting somewhere around Tasmanian Devil level. Wait until calmer times.

- Don't have BIG talks when hangry, someone is driving at speeds, when someone is manic or anxious. These situations are guaranteed to have the message misconstrued or lame during an already tense time.

- A good overall test before you say something you are concerned about will hurt the feelings of another. *"How can I make this kind?"* And *"If someone had to say this to me, what words would be most kind?"*

- If you're talking in person, try to maintain eye contact.

- If you feel that the message you're tapping out as a text message would be best delivered in person, obey that intuition and make time to see you're the person in person.

- If you're really stuck for something to say, nothing is

coming to mind, the other person is staring at you wordlessly, say, *"Thank you for sharing that with me. I'm going to collect my thoughts and come back to you on this."*

- When someone drops BIG NEWS on you and your first instinct is to shout "FUCKING BALLBAG HELLSCAPE", try instead to catch yourself and say, *"WOW! I was not expecting that. Did you see this coming?"* By getting them to expand on the news allows you, prosecutors, time to think of your next response and reinstate your jaw.

- When someone is overwhelmed, remember this classic: *"what is one thing I could do to make your life a bit easier?"*

- And, when you are stunned and don't know what to say, a good all-purpose question is, *"Wow. Can you tell me more about this?"* Gather more info and buy yourself some time to think.

It's ok to say nothing if:

- You're inebriated or under the influence of drugs.

- That you really can't do anything further.

- You don't feel you can hold your temper in check or say something without hurting another. You know you're justified in how you feel but know that making someone else's feel crap will not achieve anything meaningful.

- When the conversation has gone around and around so many times, it now ends in an endless spiral. So you choose to exit the conversation.

- The shock is so raw and visceral that you're rendered mute. You will find words in time, but right now, you're just sitting in this feeling of extreme discomfort.

If you say the wrong thing, try:

- *"I'm so sorry. I feel I said the wrong thing the other day when we met. I want to apologise to you for that"* Take note: "I apologise if you were offended by what I said" is NOT an apology. Clearly, they WERE offended as they've taken this up with you.

- *"I've thought about what I said on the call this morning, and I wish I could have a do-over on that. I don't think I clearly articulated how I feel. Are you open to me having another try at sharing how I feel?"*

- *"I was shocked by your news and said the wrong thing. I feel really bad about that. What I really want today for you to know is…."*

When you say too much:

- *"I let my mouth run away with me when we chatted. Please disregard what I said, and it was not a true representation of how I feel."*

- *"God, I really yapped on the other night. I think out was a combination of nerves and feeling vulnerable. I'm sorry I didn't allow you to have your say, and I'd like to give you a chance to do so now."*

- *"I've said more than I ought to—your turn!"*

Some other ways you can show you care without words:

- Not good face-to-face? Write a card or send a text.

- Deliver some hand-picked flowers to their door, make a meal.

And: just be together in-person. Sit. Be present. Squeeze their hand. Sometimes no words are needed.

FINAL WORDS

Since I started writing this book in 2019, in Australia, we've experienced extreme firestorms, a raging pandemic, shifting geo-political tensions including new theatres of war across the world, lockdowns, supply chain crunches, labour shortages, repeated devastating floods, a change of federal government and the rise of Amyl and the Sniffers. I'm very, very happy about two of these events (Amy and the change of Gov). The rest can get in the bin.

But through this continual upheaval and uncertainty, our words have helped heal, comfort, help and soothe. We have a choice every day to use good and kind words to bring us closer rather than divide and antagonise.

I get it wrong every day, but this book has reminded me that I can begin again tomorrow and do better. I can ask for forgiveness. I can ask for another chance to try again and bridge the divide. And I can strengthen my boundaries.

My wish for this book is that it's helped you see that your words have power—even the words you say to yourself. And you have the power to be a force for good even in the bleakest of times.

ADDITIONAL RESOURCES

If you can't be arsed typing these links into your browser just go to my webpage (www.fionajefferies.com.au) and get the direct links to these resources.

- The movie **Hunt for The Wilderpeople**. Watching this movie will cure you of gout, make you more desirable and mark you as a person of extremely discerning good taste .

- **Susan Hyatt** for self-love, activism and the most amazing heel collection. Find her at www.SHyatt.com. Sign up for her newsletters and follow her on the socials for an instant lift and "yeah, I'm kinda a big deal" vibe.

- **Carly Findlay** is a ridiculously talented activist, author and educator. She also has the best fashion on Insta and is a roller-skating maverick. Follow her on the socials to learn about what life looks like for an appearance diverse person.

- If you're in the throes of a breakup and **need assistance with financial help,** there are many good agencies and support services out there. In Australia please check out: https://www.wire.org.au (it's Victorian-based but the information is aces!)

- **Nervous about coming out?** That's totally normal but you don't need to walk this path alone. If you're in Australia please reach out to: https://au.reachout.com/articles/lgbtqi-support-services. It's a resource page that will direct you to the appropriate state-bases support service.

- **I adored this book by Aminatou Sow and Ann Freidman of Call Your Girlfriend podcast fame,** their mediation on the 2nd most important relationship after the one you have with yourself: Friendship. It was a dissection of their friendship and a love letter to friendship in general. It certainly gave me ideas on what I can do to be a better friend and how to nurture them so they continue to thrive and sustain me.

- **Leah Simmons,** founder of KAAIAA coined one of my go-to mantras. "I can do this…I AM doing this!" Check out her online classes and feel stronger, calmer and like a total badass doing the breath of fire!

- **Wondering where your money goes when you donate to a particular charity?** If you're in Australia, go here and scrutinise the chart of accounts! https://www.acnc.gov.au/charity/charities

- **Suffered harassment at work?** These are good resources if you're located in Australia: https://www.fairwork.gov.au/employment-conditions/bullying-sexual-harassment-and-discrimination-at-work/sexual-harassment-in-the-workplace

- I wrote a little of Mindy's story in I is for Illness chapter. **I think most people would benefit from a dose of Mindy.** Follow her here: https://www.mindymeiering.com

- **Want a good tune to spark your day?** Yeah, you do. Try these jealousy themed tunes:
  "Hey Jealousy" Gin Blossoms
      https://youtu.be/ah5gAkna3jI
  "Jealous Guy" Bryan Ferry
      https://youtu.be/hRzGzRqNj58
  "Ring The Alarm" Beyoncé
      https://youtu.be/eY_mrU8MPfI
  "That's Him Over There" Nina Simone
      https://youtu.be/afNlW5ezeDE
  "I'm Jealous" The Divinyls
      https://youtu.be/YiUGDE6b8oY

- **Want to know more about the "Shock and Awe Pack" I write of in Chapter 16?** Visit https://john-blake.com.au/

- In Chapter 16: Kindness, **I recommend further enquiry for white women wanting to understand the power structures that continue to uphold white supremacy to the detriment and paying of coloured people.** *Why I'm No Longer Talking to White People About Race* by Reni Eddo-Lodge is a great start for this topic. It was such a sober read for this white woman and her privilege.

- **The Digital Picnic calls itself the Nicest Place on the Internet and no lies detected.** Their CEO, Cherie Clonan values kindness and being a good human. That philosophy underpins how The Digital Picnic shows up in the world. Follow them on the socials and find ways of working with them here: https://www.thedigitalpicnic.com.au

- **If you're living in the suicide slipstream,** having recently lost someone you love, perhaps my free book A Small

Book About Suicide might offer some comfort. Get the free download here: https://www.fionajefferies.com.au/a-small-book-about-suicide/

- **Don't feel you're getting the attention you need from your health professional?** Read this: https://www.improvediagnosis.org/dxiq-column/feeling-dismissed-and-ignored-by-your-doctor-do-this/

- **What if you don't know what to say when you're supporting someone experiencing grief?** This article by Jan Richardson gives a first-person account of what was meaningful to her: https://wildgrief.org/blog/what-to-say-when-there-are-no-words

- If you're having youtube getting your bebe to go the fuck to sleep, **Tool have got your back:** https://open.spotify.com/album/7zp3rUAqmTmbbpodPXmwKe?si=LWiZP9ccT0qrM_3f1KRiIg. (It also works to soothe adults to sleep)

- **Want to quit?** Why not start with social media. The very brilliant Alexandra Franzen has written on reasons to give up the 'Gram. http://www.alexandrafranzen.com/2021/03/15/quit/

- "Um, Satan?" "Yes, Joanne" **"I'm feeling particularly ragey today. Got ideas?"** Indeed I do: https://www.tiktok.com/@stanzipotenza?lang=en

- **The secret history of single ladies is a fascinating read.** Read how unmarried women are rising and rising. https://www.booktopia.com.au/all-the-single-ladies-rebecca-traister/book/9781476716572.html

❋ Want a dose of Mary's solo living and loving it? Go here and soak in the joy of having a room (or rooms!) of one's own: https://youtu.be/ZNKOt2k7Pm4

❋ I've lived in flats and apartments most of my adult life and the VERY close living with neighbours is both cool and rage-inducing. In one particular home, I suffered more than any woman should with regular drink and drug nights that always coincided with my having to get up early either for rowing or to catch a flight. The sound of a bunch of drunken yobs playing Beer Pong to the small hours and then at 1 am announcing "Pass me the machete Paul, I'm cutting down the palm tree"—well, let's just say the palm tree was remarkably resistant and stood tall. Until the next party. Every time I hear these songs it reminds me of all those drunken, drug-fuelled nights as I tried to jam plugs in my ears to get sleep and having to call an ambulance because one of the party-goers decided to scale the outside of the apartment high on meth, lose their footing and land spine-first onto the pebble-create below. Roll tape! Break on Through to the Otherside by The Doors: https://youtu.be/rOpQjD-rX0g. Hits from The Bong by Cypress Hill: https://youtu.be/xyqVVfj5qE8. And this song was once put on repeat at a party for **FIVE FUCKING HOURS. PEOPLE, THIS IS REASON ALONE NOT TO DO DRUGS. THESE MUSIC CHOICES ARE NOT FOR YOUR HIGHER GOOD:** "Itchycoo Park" by The Small Faces https://youtu.be/fayL1WTR1Go

❋ **I'm a worker archetype in the money quiz but what are you?** Try out the quiz here: https://thefemalemoneydoctor.com/sma-quiz/

✺ **NEED!** Marimekko cushions: https://livingbydesign.net.au/collections/marimekko-cushions?gclid=EAIaIQobChMItf-N2dmB-AIVB5lmAh1OyQs-DEAAYASAAEgLrd_D_BwE

✺ **Share a meal!** Let's make some tacos and salsa the night away. https://www.donnahay.com.au/recipes/s/chipotle-chicken-and-cauliflower-tacos

✺ **This song will make you catch your breath every time.** It's a powerful reminder that we're stronger together: https://youtu.be/GpsAy0kSiE8

✺ I don't care if you're an employer or employee, **you can learn and laugh from Jen's Workplace Newsletter.** The best part is: you realise every workplace has issues like yours. But hopefully, Jen can give you advice and tips that steers you away from being shirt-fronted at legal tribunal: https://jenniferbicknell.com.au

✺ **Let's get low-level scandalised!** "Imagination" by Belouis Some: https://youtu.be/ZmD0ZArJfJQ / "Girls On Film" by Duran Duran: https://youtu.be/KCjMZMxNr-0 "Justify My Love" by Madonna https://youtu.be/Np_Y740aReI

✺ **A website aimed at kids and thor supporters going through tough times:** https://headspace.org.au

✺ **Need a good read?** Try this! It unpacks the QAnon conspiracy methodically and is a gripping read. I mean, where is the floor under this level of delusion?!? QAnon and On by Van Badham. https://www.amazon.com.au/QAnon-Shocking-History-Internet-Conspiracy/dp/1743797877

ACKNOWLEDGEMENTS

The absolute A-Team of book production services gave me the support, love and gentle reminders to keep going even when it was the 16th time I wanted to trash it all. Lindsey, Alex, Woz, Andrew, Lucy, Kayla, and Tracie are the very best book doulas. I love youse all. I look forward to giving you each an uncomfortably long hug when I see you in person.

Andrea, Shirley, Suzanne, Cate, Renai, Emma, Karyn, Dixie, Soraya, Tory, Becca, Dave, Lizzie, Kevin, Rosemary, Donna, Shona... I've been so lucky to have you in my life. Thank you for providing so much inspiration for saying good words—big love.

Mum, Dad, Emma, Phil Cate, Amy, Archie, Aunty Christine and Uncle Steve—big thanks for being there for me, always.

The Divas. Massive thanks for giving me a forum each and every day to say good words beyond taking a deep exhale and sying "Fuuuuuuuuccccckkkkk".

I would not have written this book without chocolate and burgers. Not necessarily together.

This book got written in so many locations, but my favourite was The Alcott Pub (a seat outside on the deck, thanks) and a divine BnB at Bar Beach (thank you, Janet, for your magical space!)

I really think the role of good music is highly underrated as a soundtrack to writing. Here's to you, Emma Donovan and the Pushbacks, Lana Del Rey, Nine Inch Nails, Patti Smith, Amyl and the Sniffers, Olympia, Lizzo, Tool, The Snowy Band, Henry Rollins, and You Am I.

And finally, to my man-friend G. Words will never be enough for how I feel about you and how you've added so much MORE to my life. So I shall perform it as an interpretive dance instead.

ENDNOTES

1. By fine, I mean friends, family and known associates that are fine with me swearing like I've got my tits jammed in the fridge door.

2. **ANZUS TREATY.** In 1951, an agreement between Australia, New Zealand and the USA was signed to protect the security of The Pacific. It still stands to this day. Although when Trump was elected president of the USA in 2016, please know that there was a generous amount of side-eye happening and scanning for escape clauses in the Treaty. Please, our American Eagle friends, less of the fascist bully-boy and more of the rock n' roll.

3. This line is of course from the brilliant and funny "Hunt for the Wilderpeople". Please stop whatever you're doing and watch this movie immediately. It will cure what ails ya.

4. Incidentally, I ran out of fuck's-I-have-to-give in 2013 when our cretinous male Prime Minister of Australia, Tony Abbott made himself the Minister for Women in our federal cabinet, despite a. Not being a woman and b. Doing all he could to devalue and add hardship to the lives of women by defunding women's shelters, refusing to promote women to cabinetry positions and generally being a sexist god-botherer. Tool.

5   It's a blanket ban here. Nothing good can come out of a bunch of 11-year-old undercooked musicians destroying Taylor Swift's "Shake it off" at the school assembly. I've grasped that the only way to get better at something is to practise but you don't have to rope in 600 good citizens each and every term to sit through such caterwauling. I mean, we're several years into a pandemic, will the pain never stop?

6   No judgment. I've heard about sister wives and those weird free-love communes where everyone dresses in hessian sacks and no one owns a comb. And even in this commune that bill itself as a sexual utopia, we STILL get the bullshit where women do all the household chores, carries the invisible load and the men get to lay around, scratch their balls through hemp pants and do fuck all.

7   And while I'm on this bent, kombucha is just bullshit for anything. Something that ranks with a sedimentary vibe is not meant for human consumption. Good god, the toxic Cockle Creek in Newcastle, where I grew up, is cleaner and tastier than the average kombucha! Kombucha is just virtue signalling for the too earnest, overwrought influencer set who are trying to shill shit. Resist!

8   To anyone who had given me grief about arriving at an airport so far ahead of time it's laughable—get bent, being early has its own rewards.

9   Songwriters: Paul David Hewson / Adam Clayton / Larry Mullen / Dave Evans
    One lyrics © Polygram Int. Music Publishing B.v.

CPSIA information can be obtained
at www.ICGtesting.com
Printed in the USA
BVHW040428171022
649227BV00002B/20

9 780645 628418